I'll never forget the day I met Kurt. I love what I do with the Fellowship of Christian Athletes, and I've realized through this ministry, I am privileged to meet not just athletes and coaches, but the great supporters of these competitors—trainers, managers, school administrators, etc. The funny thing is I never considered Kurt a competitor until we talked. He was just the trainer on the golf cart, right?

Kurt is an inspiration! As I read his book, I found myself lingering in my past, connecting with his stories, one after another! Maybe because I'm a Hoosier, or maybe because I have experienced life challenges, this book was encouraging and motivating.

One of my favorite quotes from his book, "My SMA battle chose me; I did not choose it. But only I could choose the path this battle would take me down. Every day is a struggle, but every day I choose to continue the fight." Kurt is a competitor and a fighter! It makes sense that his occupation matches his heart as he strives to help others and keep them in the field of play.

Kurt has discovered his purpose in life, and as you read this book, you will be challenged to find your purpose too.

Rex Stump
Fellowship of Christian Athletes

SEARCHING FOR EVERY STEP

FINDING PURPOSE IN LIVING WITH SPINAL MUSCULAR ATROPHY

KURT E.BEACH

Searching with Every Step: Finding Purpose in Living with Spinal Muscular Atrophy
Published by Beach Publishing. LLC.
Perrysburg, OH

ISBN: 978-0-578-97197-1
BIOGRAPHY & AUTOBIOGRAPHY / Personal Memoirs
SELF-HELP / Motivational & Inspirational

Cover and Interior design by Victoria Wolf, wolfdesignandmarketing.com. Copyright owned by Kurt Beach.

 BEACH PUBLISHING

*I would like to dedicate this book to just
a few important people in my life.*

First would be my parents for always showing me the right way to live. For showing me that strength, fortitude, and giving are all the traits that we need. For my mom for showing me Jesus and for always being there for me at my highest highs and lowest lows. You have always been an ear to listen to me whenever I need it. For my dad for teaching me to love all people and sometimes to drop what you're doing when a friend needs a hand.

To Mikayla and Colton. Someday, I hope you read this back to your children to show them what kind of grandfather they had. I hope I have shown you the same strength and resilience that my parents have shown me and that no matter what happens in life, just keep moving forward and never let anyone stand in your way of achieving what you want.

To my beautiful wife. Thank you for always being there for me and never giving up on me. You have shown me what true love is about. You have given me everything that I have ever wished for as my wife. I will forever be your love.

INTRODUCTION

WHEN I GOT OFF THE PLANE midday in Ft. Lauderdale, the first thing that hit me was the humidity. It immediately fogged up my glasses and instantly made me want to take my sweatpants off and get into a pair of shorts. The second was the torrential afternoon downpour. A tropical storm seemed to be rolling in, and the wind was intense enough to make me question the sanity of being here to launch a kayak into the open ocean and bike for about 120 miles— which I would be doing over the next three days as part of the Project Athena Keys to Recovery Adventure.

An adventure with Keys to Recovery in its title doesn't sound like it could be a bad adventure, does it? Especially an adventure that takes you through sunny Florida? And in November? That's what I thought when I first heard about this "adventure"—at a time when, where I lived in Toledo, Ohio, the temperature had already dropped to below forty-five degrees for the high of the day and would dip into the twenties and thirties at night. The friend who recommended it and the website made it sound like a nice three-day vacation hopping into a kayak and paddling ten to thirteen miles a day with a nice thirty-mile daily bike ride to go along with it—all with a group of like-minded outdoor enthusiasts celebrating life. I was in!

Enthusiasm flagged as I told people what I would be doing, and I watched their eyes run the gamut from sad to deer in the headlights to a "no way would I want to do that" look. But I was clear on my purpose. Besides, this was not a vacation but was more of a business trip. I had some work to accomplish to prove something to myself. Physically, yes, but also an intangible something I needed to find out.

The Project Athena Foundation (PAF) is a nonprofit organization based out of California. It was founded by Robyn Benincasa, a 2014 CNN hero and veteran Ironman Triathlon finisher who survived a medical setback and started the foundation to support others. During her evolution from young competitive gymnast then collegiate diving athlete to firefighter and racer, she discovered that the longer the race, the stronger the fire she had. Eventually, she found adventure racing to be the sport she loved.

Robyn's love led to her doing more than forty adventure races in the Eco-Challenge series, which became a popular TV show produced by Marc Burnett (the originator of the CBS *Survivor*) in the 1990s on Discovery Channel. Teams of four or five individuals dropped into the middle of nowhere had the goal to finish the competition faster than the other teams. With the average event being over 300 miles, each team would have to navigate by maps and compasses (that's right, no GPS) through a series of checkpoints to the finish. The only way to navigate the course was through man-powered means (biking, hiking, swimming, kayaking, paddle boarding, repelling, etc.). Each team had to stay within fifty meters of each other, and if one person had to drop out or became injured, the team would be disqualified. Robyn led her team to two wins and placed on the podium twenty times in the series.

One day in the middle of a race at the World Championships, she began to develop pain in her hips. Pushing to finish as much as she could, not to disappoint her team, she crossed the finish line, literally by picking up her legs with her hands to move her forward due to pain. After flying back to the United States, Jeff, her fiancé (and eventually husband), had to lift her out of her plane seat and carry her to the car and home. Her diagnosis was that she had stage IV osteoarthritis in both of her hips, and she would never be able to run again.

She drew encouragement in this devastating time from her close friend Louise Cooper, who was battling breast cancer but was not allowing the cancer to take her life. Louise put things on her calendar to achieve—simple things like walking down to the curb to get the paper—so she always put a goal in front of her.

Robyn followed suit and found the drive in herself to do the same, leaning on her strong suits of paddle boarding and kayaking. (She earned three Guinness World Records for Farthest Distance kayaking and stand-up paddle boarding by a female.) You can read more about Robyn in her New York Times best seller, *How Winning Works,* and about the foundation at ProjectAthena.org.

She set up the foundation to support people who had a medical or physical setback in their lives and were ready for a comeback. An adventure dream was part of their recovery, so the foundation has hosted several adventures. The one I signed up for, Keys to Recovery, covers 120 miles, traveling by bike and kayak, over three days from Key Largo, Florida, to Key West (the southernmost part of the continental United States).

I knew I wouldn't be meeting up with the other participants until the following morning. Since my travel was arranged by the foundation, I knew I would have a roommate, but I had no idea who it was or when he would arrive. Two other participants reached out with dinner invitations before the trip, but several sleepless nights and an early morning departure have left me too exhausted to join in just yet. Instead, I got my bags, made my way to the hotel, and tuned into some mindless competition on the Food Network.

As I cleared my mind for the first time that day, I took note that I would turn forty-four on the middle day of the three-day adventure, feeling just that old and simultaneously as if something inside of me was being birthed—with all the emotions of anticipation, fear, and excitement of a young boy. I also carried the added weight of a diagnosis from age eighteen of a rare neuromuscular condition known as spinal muscular atrophy (SMA)—and all the fears about my body and stamina that have dogged me since I received that diagnosis twenty-five years ago.

The looming question I had was, *How did I get here?*

CHAPTER I

THE DIAGNOSIS

"ALL ATHLETES ARE DISCIPLINED in their training. They do it to win a prize that will fade away, but we do it for an eternal prize. So I run with purpose in every step. I am not just shadowboxing. I discipline my body like an athlete, training it to do what it should. Otherwise, I fear that after preaching to others I myself might be disqualified" (1 Corinthians 9). This verse written by Paul captures my life perfectly, although I can't say I was aware of it until after the Project Athena adventure. I did discipline my body like an athlete, and I searched with every step for purpose and God's plan for my life.

My pivot point when my life irrevocably changed occurred after high school graduation. It came in the form of a medical setback that could have been permanently debilitating if I had accepted my doctor's diagnosis. I had always loved sports and had participated with enthusiasm if not discipline to the best of my abilities as part of school teams in basketball and golf, and recreational league baseball.

Before entering college, I needed a mandatory physical examination. My prior physicals were normal and unmemorable, except for the moments when the doctor put on his pair of rubber gloves, snapped the end band around his wrist, and said, "Go ahead and drop your pants." This time it was different.

One of the things my mom and I wanted to definitively discuss with Dr. Peterson was my inability and lack of strength to be able to run fast or even run, period. I wasn't the most in-shape I could have been. Well, let's just be honest—I was kind of lazy with my physical activity and resisted doing anything extra throughout the last four years of my high school career. I knew going into college that I had to take a physical education class and that most of the classes those days were graded on performance and how much one improved over the semester. My brother, Kevin, and I knew that neither of us could run well, and we did not want to be docked for our shortcomings.

A few times in high school, Kevin and I were sent to physical therapy to help strengthen our muscles in our legs and relieve pain. This time, late in summer right before college, Dr. Peterson took us through the same battery of musculoskeletal tests as previous examinations, from walking, squatting, and sitting on a chair to standing and getting up and down off the floor. After he was finished, he looked at my mom and said for the first time, "I think we should look into this further with an expert in neuromuscular disorders." With preparations for college looming over me, I thought little of it over the next few weeks until we headed down to Indianapolis to see a neurologist who might have been able to give us an answer. When I noticed a sign next to the doors we entered that said Muscular Dystrophy Association (MDA) clinic, a stab of fear and gloom hit me.

What I knew of muscular dystrophy (MD) came from watching the Jerry Lewis telethon religiously with my parents every Labor Day weekend. Jerry Lewis and Dean Martin were well-known for their off-the-wall comedies and other exploits during the 1950s. In 1966, Jerry Lewis joined up with the MDA to host an eighteen-hour telethon, starting the night before Labor Day and running through most of Monday to help raise money to find a cure for muscular dystrophy. I loved listening to all the singers and entertainers they provided and was moved by the sad stories people told of their physical and mental hardships and struggles. And I was warmed and excited by the victories some of the families shared and how much money was raised every year for research.

The pain of MD was in the back of my mind as Kevin and I completed the series of tests, including lots of blood work, a muscle biopsy, and neurological examinations that seemed to last all day. I noticed everything the doctors did during the neuromuscular tests, called the Hammersmith neurological exam, which were originally used to detect a related condition called spinal muscular atrophy. Part of the exam involved doing muscular activities—flipping over coins, tearing a piece of paper, climbing steps, getting off the ground from a kneeling position—designed to assess the function of my upper and lower extremities: shoulders, arms, hands, and wrists plus everything from hip to toe.

Being the competitor that I am, I fought my hardest to do all the tests and try to be perfect on each one. But as we went along, the tests got harder and harder, finally becoming too difficult to complete.

My brother and I got separated and were given the option between two tests. My brother chose the EMG, where they inserted a giant needle into the belly muscles then made him contract muscles while they read the activity. Seeing the pain that caused my brother, I was relieved I had chosen the other test where I was put on a table and numbed in the middle of my thigh so they could go in and take a biopsy of the tissue. We left the clinic exhausted, confused, and sore. We were told nothing about the results or possibilities.

Kevin and I attended Ball State University, which was close enough that we were commuting from home. We started classes, but the cloud of wondering what my tests results were hovered over my head. Eventually, the time came to drive back to the clinic, where my brother, mom, and I sat in the waiting room patiently waiting to see the physician. The doctor finally called us back and broke the news.

Optimistically, I was hoping for the best because I wasn't sure of the extent of the worst. He went on to explain to us that the fibers in our muscles were significantly smaller than in normal muscles, and that all they could tell us was that the nerves weren't getting the complete signal to the muscles, causing them to atrophy. He said this condition is known as spinal muscular atrophy (SMA).

Recalling our awkwardness and lack of speed and jumping ability, plus the many times I tripped over things while walking, not only skinning my knees but also ruining many pairs of pants, it all started to make sense. I also remembered the numerous times I developed knee pain after playing basketball and being so tired after games and practices, and the painful, cruel times when kids came up behind Kevin and me as a joke and clipped the back of our knees to watch us fall to the ground because we could not catch ourselves. It also explained the times we would be so strong on the front nine holes of a golf course, then along the back half no matter how hard we tried, we both would suffer.

I remembered from watching the Jerry Lewis telethon that SMA was one of the rare syndromes of the MD family. Only one in 10,000 people are born with this condition and six out of ten of those children born with it have type one, which leads to early death before the age of one year. The neurologist said our case was even rarer because our symptoms developed later in life and there was no certainty of when and how this disease would progress for both of us.

After he had finished explaining everything about how he wanted to check in with us every six months to monitor our condition, I asked him the question I was afraid to know the answer to. I told him my brother and I were attending college and were thinking of careers as athletic trainers, and I wanted to know if we could continue with our plans. Without hesitating, he said, "You should look into getting a career where you can work at a desk, because with this condition, you'll likely be in a wheelchair by the time you're thirty-five." I sat statuesque as I absorbed the words and their paralyzing power. Many years later, I was asked if I remembered much about my surroundings in that room that day or even what my neurologist looked like or more importantly what his name was. I hardly remember a thing except for three points: this is the disease that you have, we don't know what causes it, and finally, there is no cure or treatment for it as of now. But the one thing that I remember the most was those words telling me to give up something I knew I wanted to become. The power of those words would shift in my life from numbing to motivating as I fought to prove the doctor wrong, and they strengthened me in my search for purpose in my life.

I also remember looking over at my mom and seeing her tear up at not knowing how she could fix this. Mom was always the one who helped Kevin and me get through hard times. She always had the right thing to say when we were sad, nervous, angry, happy, or terrified, and she always knew how to fix situations and make them right. When we had issues with schoolwork or relationships, she was always the one who was there to give us a hand or think of a way to solve the issues. This time, she just sat there, waiting, as dazed as we were. All I wanted to do in that moment was ask her, "What do we need to do, Mom, to fix this?"

But even then, I sensed it was going to be up to me and only me to figure out how to handle this for myself. How was I going to change this path? How was I going to make this better? How was I going to live my life and live into my future? Even though I knew I had my parents, friends, and even some sense of God in my life, that knowledge receded, and it was the first time I felt truly alone.

CHAPTER 2

ALL IN THE FAMILY

I GREW UP AS A "NORMAL" child after being born at Ball Memorial Hospital in a small town about an hour north of Indianapolis. The town gets a mention by country singer Toby Keith in his song "I Wanna Talk About Me." Yep, that's right, Muncie, Indiana. We actually lived out in the country near an even smaller town, Gaston, on the northwest side of Delaware County. So, to say I had a small-town kind of living is an understatement.

I like to compare my birth to the first time I was in line for the Gatekeeper roller coaster in Cedar Point amusement park over in Ohio. I am sure my mom's pregnancy with me felt like standing in line for a long time. For me, it was a thirty-seven-week vacation in a nice warm "Beach" (our last name) near the ocean. At the Gatekeeper ride, it was slow moving until I could step up behind the yellow line with gates on three sides that could finally be unlocked by the attendant to allow me on the ride. You know that person slouching in his chair is a twenty-one-year-old college student who was probably out partying with his friends the night before and probably had minimal sleep. But he's the one who pushes the red button to swing the gate open that is keeping you safe and cozy. As that gate opens, his voice comes over the loud speaker: "Please step forward and welcome to the Gatekeeper." Excitement explodes in me after anticipating crossing that line and entering a new world for so long—excitement and fear, not knowing what to expect on the other side.

It was the same for me in my mother's womb the day I was born. I don't know if I was ready, but the gate opened, and it was my turn. My mother says she thinks I got a foot in her back the minute that gate opened. And she got a different ride than she expected too. My parents had seen the ultrasound back in the 1970s, when the technology was not as accurate as it is now. Today you can see hands and feet and even make three-dimensional pictures of a child still in the womb. At the time, though, my parents were informed with certainty they were having one child. But after my shove in my back as the coaster gate opened, a second passenger came through who would be going on this ride of life together with me.

That's right; I'm a twin. As the doctor was finishing taking care of me, he got a surprise and told my mom, who also thought she was done, that there was another one coming. My mom said, "No, that should not be. I was only supposed to have one." He replied to her in a strong voice, "Well, today you're having two." During birth, my mother's water had broken twice, which now made sense. But she assumed that two sacs meant two different eggs and Kevin and I were fraternal twins. My dad was equally surprised when the doctor exited the delivery room and told him he was the proud father of two healthy baby boys. My dad almost choked and asked, "What did you say?" Yep, two boys. My dad and mom, though I'm sure they were proud, were also thinking, "Okay, but what we will do with two?"

That time was not easy for my parents from what they tell me. For those of you reading this who might have twins, you know what I am talking about. You feed one kid, and as soon as you're done getting him changed and back to sleep, the other one wakes up, and you must do it all over again. Now try doing laundry and cleaning and all that while taking care of those two needy kids. My parents were also both working. Mom taught third grade at Grissom Elementary (on the south side of Muncie School District), and my dad was head supervisor at the Warner Gear transmission plant.

For me, however, being a twin was great. Throughout my childhood, I never had to worry about someone to play with. It was like having a mirror looking back at me. We pretty much did the same things together all the time. My mom used to say if one of us was playing in the toilet, the other one was climbing in the drawers at the same time. But even though we were so much alike, I always knew there was something different about both of us. That just took some time for both of us to figure out.

As a toddler, I lifted my head, rolled over, sat up, pulled myself up, and walked. Even so, my parents were always extra protective of my brother and me. To be fair, we did give them some cause to be wary. Three days after birth, for example, my mom was doing "this little piggy went to market." She didn't get past "this little piggy stayed home" when she noticed that both our second and third toes were hooked together. She rushed us to the ER worrying there was something wrong. As the doctor came in, he took one look and said nothing was wrong other than "your boys will be good swimmers." (Kevin and I did end up loving the water and spent hours at the pool starting at age four with swimming classes. But when my mom noticed we were not enjoying them, she let us learn on our own. So, yes, we could swim, but we were nowhere near being good swimmers.)

The first two years of our lives, we were frequent fliers to the ER. One time I was told that I could go outside and was so excited, I started running toward the door to the backyard. After a few steps, I tripped and ran my whole hand through the large window next to the door, breaking the glass and ripping off a huge chunk of my skin. My dad had to hold a towel on it to stop the bleeding and keep my hand connected on the drive to the hospital. I have the scar on my wrist to mark the incident.

Another night, Mom called out it was time for baths, and Kevin and I ran from opposite sides of the house toward the bathroom. We rounded the corner at the same time and ran into each other. Kevin got sent to the ER for stitches in his chin. I also sent him to the ER when we were four after I rolled up the car window on his finger. The finger eventually swelled up over the top of his nail bed. Still today, he doesn't have to cut that nail and calls it his screwed-up finger.

By the time we got to grade school, life got a little easier for my parents. Kevin and I were separated into different classrooms from first through fifth grade, because my mom discovered when we were in preschool that we each were able to recite only half of the alphabet (plus we had the same girlfriend in preschool). My mom figured this out when she was going over the ABCs with us, and I looked at Kevin and told him, "that is your half." From that point on, we were separated, so we would have to learn everything by ourselves.

My parents were a study in opposites. My mother grew up in the small town of Logansport, Indiana, in the middle of farm country with my Grandma and Grandpa Scott and my uncle Scotty (his first name was Everett but for some reason he was always Uncle Scotty to me; I never knew why). My mom played the clarinet and was able to play in the Indianapolis 500 Parade, which was a big achievement for her. That luster didn't fade even though she had to walk the entire black asphalt track (2.5 miles around) in the blazing sun on Memorial Day weekend before the big car race. My mom helped my grandpa on the farm—other than when she was trying to get away from her brother, who often chased her around the farmhouse with a BB gun, trying to shoot her in the behind. After high school, my mom decided to become a teacher and attended what was called back then Indiana Teachers College (now Ball State). She kept her love of music and, in addition to playing the piano, directed our church youth choir whenever we would put on a play at Christmas and in Vacation Bible School. When I was in third grade, my dad bought her a piano for Christmas with cash he made selling his woodworking projects—like crosses, bowls, and figurines—that he stashed in a can by their bed.

My father, on the other hand, was a born-and-raised Muncie city boy who lived near downtown. He was a student at Muncie Central High School but never really played sports. Well, he tried his freshman year until the football coach told him he had to run the stairs during the first week of practice. My dad threw the football at him and told him he "could stick it where the sun don't shine." (Knowing my dad, those were probably not the exact words that were said, but you get the gist.) That was the last day my dad played any organized sport in high school. His father, Grandpa Beach, was a police officer, and from what I remember of my dad's stories, he was one tough guy—not one you would want to mess around with.

When he was not at the Muncie Fieldhouse watching basketball or at the stadium watching football, you could find him at the local railroad tracks, especially after a rainy day, shooting at frog air sacs—that bladder that blows up when a male frog breathes. Yep, that would be my dad. And even though my dad didn't play sports, he was a Muncie Central High Bearcat through and through. We joked that if they cut my dad, he would bleed the Central colors of purple and white. After high school, he entered the workforce starting on the line at BorgWarner automotive plant. He had joined the labor union and eventually would become a head supervisor at the transmission plant, known for treating his employees as equals. I think his drive for equality arose because he was in his employees' shoes early on in his career.

One of my favorite stories my dad told was about the labor union strikes at BorgWarner automotive. Whenever the labor union went on strike, they would camp outside the fences of the transmission plant. Bottles and other objects occasionally would get thrown at the other supervisors and higher-ups as they rolled into work. Though there were no employees working every day, my dad still had to report. As my dad would approach the gate, every man there would stop yelling or throwing stuff and beckon to my dad, "Hey, Beach, come have a doughnut and coffee with us."

My dad was twenty-three when he met my mom, who was nineteen years old and still in college. They met at my mom's sorority house at a party a friend of my dad's invited him to. My father had been recently divorced from the mother of my half-sister, Tammy. I am sure there was something that intrigued him about this sweet country girl from Logansport. They dated for months and eventually tied the knot.

Times were hard for both of my parents after they married. My dad was dealing with a messy situation concerning Tammy, who was flown around the world with her mom and barely was allowed to see her dad (my dad) most of her life. I am sure hardly ever getting to spend time with his daughter was rough for him, but he never showed it, or much emotion in general. When times got tough, you would never know it with him.

Working for the union at the transmission plant threw my dad constant curve balls. Many times, he was laid off due to down production. But my parents always found a way to make the finances work. In those times, my dad would try to pick up odd jobs to do, like construction and maintaining grave stones at a cemetery. One night my mom and dad went to a dance place for a date with just $1.50 on hand. They sat down at a table and were able to get a bag of chips and a soda, which they shared as they listened to the local band play. They did not need much besides each other at the time—and that was the point.

I remember that story because that was the way I was raised. Hard times are a given in life, and life will throw you curve balls sometimes when all you really want is a fast ball straight down the middle. We were taught that even in the rough times of life, you have each other—not only your family but also your faith. My parents' lives had their ups and downs, with exciting times and scary times. But they always had faith that, through hunkering down together and getting the job at hand done, God was watching out for them and they'd be okay, no matter the circumstances.

We all know the line, "Life is like a box of chocolates. You never know what you are going to get," delivered by Tom Hanks as Forrest

Gump in the 1994 movie. He was talking to a nurse sitting on a bench near a bus stop about his philosophy of life, which he compared to a box of chocolate candies that look the same on the outside and hid what might come next when you bit into them. He seemed to like the not knowing. I'd have to say I'm the opposite. I hate looking at a box of chocolates I might have received for Valentine's Day or maybe even Christmas and trying to guess what I would get. I hated the coconut and cherry ones, and eight times out of ten, the first one I picked was, you guessed it, coconut or cherry. So I wanted to know what was coming and be able to avoid getting what I didn't want. In the same way, I managed my condition to avoid getting hurt.

CHAPTER 3

FOR THE LOVE
OF SPORTS

I COME BY MY LOVE OF SPORTS naturally from my parents and from growing up in Indiana. Hoosier Hysteria is a real thing. The inventor of basketball, James Naismith, said in 1925, "While the game was invented in Massachusetts, basketball really had its origin in Indiana, which remains the center of the sport." The first game was played in the year 1891 with two peach baskets placed along the railings in the small gym. There were nine players on each team, and the only way they could advance the ball was to pass it to someone on their team. Over time, the rules of his game evolved. A protégé of Naismith's brought the game back to his YMCA gym in Crawfordsville, Indiana. The first reported game there was on

November 17, 1894, between the Crawfordsville and the Lafayette YMCAs. News traveled fast, and Indiana basketball was born. It became known throughout the countryside, as basketball hoops were nailed to the side of barns where kids could play. In 1911, the first Indiana state tournament was born.

What is the one thing a Hoosier is known for? Basketball. Being a native Indianan, I always said you were born and raised to play basketball until you know you don't have what it takes to play. When Kevin and I started playing, my father had a concrete court placed in our backyard along with a hoop and a floodlight that lit up the entire court so my friends could come over and we could play at all hours.

My brother and I dabbled in our grade school years, playing weekend games over at the high school during the winter season after baseball was done. Playing in the rec league every Sunday was the highlight of my weekend. Kevin and I were among the taller kids in our age group, and it was easier for both of us to reach up higher than most of the other kids. I'm not going to lie—there were many over-the-backboard passes, either to myself or to Kevin—we also would get plenty of over-the-back calls. I was able to secure a bunch of rebounds, even though at that age, putting the ball back in the hoop was more like a volleyball game between Kevin and me than basketball. Because of our height, we didn't need to jump much, which was a good thing because neither of us could jump very high. My parents said it looked like we had concrete in our shoes.

And wearing those short shorts—exposing my long, skinny legs—was not going to win me any leg modeling contracts. One older kid was just as tall as we were, but height did not equal speed. Among the three of us, we also were not going to win any sprinting events, that's for sure. We could run up and down the court with enthusiasm, but for the most part, the ball got held quite often so we could catch up with everyone and they could start the play. Overall, I loved basketball, and it is still one of my favorite sports I ever played.

Many times, we found ourselves over at Muncie Central Fieldhouse watching basketball. Well, more accurately, while my parents sat a few rows from the top of the gym, Kevin and I played games with some of the younger kids while the varsity games were going on. I have always loved the atmosphere that that gymnasium held and its rich history.

During my youth until 1997, for all sports besides football, there was a one-class system, meaning all schools in the state tournament for basketball played each other no matter the size of the school. This is memorialized in the movie *Hoosiers*. Gene Hackman plays the role of a retired coach who is brought to a small Indiana farm school to coach the basketball team. The school, with a total enrollment of 161 kids, is pitted against a school of more than 1,662 for the Indiana state title and, spoiler alert, the win. Despite the possibility, that match-up and result rarely happened, but in the year 1954, a young man named Bobby Plump from Milan High School did hit the game-winning shot to beat the bigger school, Muncie Central, for the state title. My father was a third-grader at the time and remembers that game quite well.

Though saddened the Bearcats did not win that year, my dad had plenty of opportunity to see his beloved Bearcats win a state title. In 1988, Chandler "Showtime" Thompson was a senior for the Bearcats. He had already committed to play at Ball State the following year. Rick Majerus was a longtime, well-known coach who recruited Thompson but left Ball State to coach at Utah in 1989. That year, the Ball State Cardinals, under new head coach Dick Hunsaker and Thompson, advanced to the Sweet Sixteen, becoming the first Mid-American Conference team to ever reach that far. However, there they had to face the eventual national champions, the UNLV Runnin' Rebels (coached by legendary Jerry Tarkanian, famous for the wet towel he used to chew on and stash underneath his seat) and lost 69–67. In the last seconds, Muncie Central's own Chandler Thompson had the opportunity to tie the game but missed the shot. The highlight of that game in my mind was Chandler's put-back dunk over multiple UNLV players.

The 1988 Bearcats were coached by another legend, Bill Harrell (the basketball court at the fieldhouse is now named after him), and the team had only one loss going into the state tournament. The sectional title game, which was played at the fieldhouse every year, was where we Beaches were. Yep, top row of a packed gym, to see the Bearcats play their cross-town rivals, the Muncie Southside Rebels. The Bearcats won that game in the closing minutes, 66–61. Watching the student body rush the court after their team won was such an amazing sight for me as a sixth grader. The team eventually played at the famous Anderson High School Wigwam for the regional title then at Hinkle Fieldhouse on the Butler University campus in Indianapolis (showcased in *Hoosiers*), where they won the semi-state title.

The Muncie Central basketball team and its' four police car escorts traveled to the state final four games at Market Square Arena in Indianapolis (where the Indiana Pacers played until 1999). The semifinal game was against Bedford North Lawrence, and they faced the future Indiana University Hall of Famer, Damon Bailey, who was just a sophomore at the time. Muncie won that game too, 60–53. (Two years later, Bailey would lead his team to the

1990 state title then go on to have a great career for Bobby Knight at Indiana University.)

The Indiana High School Athletic Association (IHSAA) state title game was played the next day between Muncie and the Concord Minutemen before a sold-out crowd of 17,940. The undefeated Minutemen were led by future NBA All-Star and franchise player for the Seattle Supersonics Shawn Kemp. Kemp fouled out with three minutes and forty-eight seconds left in the game, having scored twenty-three points and grabbing thirteen rebounds. But the Muncie Central Bearcats were triumphant once again, winning 76–53 for their eighth basketball title in state history as a one-class system. That record stands today as the most state titles of any sport in Indiana history. I watched that championship game on television while listening to Morry Mannies' radio broadcast with amazement. I, too, wanted to participate in a thrilling championship game like that and earn a medal someday.

My dad was also excited to see his Bearcats win. It was late at night, but as soon as the game ended, he frantically searched for his Bearcat sweatshirt to put on, grabbed his hat, and was out the door. That night, he went over to the fieldhouse for a post-game celebration when the basketball team got back to Muncie from Indianapolis. I stayed home with my mother and brother but saw the pictures of the celebration the next morning on the front page in the *Muncie Star Press*. To see that gym packed with people in a sea of purple and white was unforgettable. The night before, when the game was over, I was especially struck by the IHSAA president going down the line of the Muncie basketball team and draping each player with a medal in the shape of the state of Indiana around their necks. In the newspaper photo, the team was standing around the Indiana map outline with the IHSAA logo engraved in the center, each one proudly wearing his medal. The writing under the logo read, "1988 State Boys Basketball Champion." Seeing those medals and how excited my dad was about that game inspired me. I wanted my dad to see me winning a championship medal someday. This was my Hoosier dream!

Before basketball, there was baseball. Our parents started Kevin and me early with T-ball. Obviously at age six, no one is good, and the only thing you worry about is picking dandelions in the outfield. Then if, and only if, a ball comes out into the outfield, you run after it as fast as you can. It wasn't until we got to third grade that things got to be more competitive. At this level, every kid wanting to play in the major leagues had to try out by batting, running, and fielding. I remember that I wasn't the worst and I wasn't the best. Being twins, Kevin and I were picked for the same team, and given our last name was Beach, we quickly became the Beach Boys, which I always thought had a nice ring to it. During that time, we were not the fittest of all athletes, but every time we went up to the plate, we wanted to be that person who hit it over the fence and made it all the way around the bases. In reality, most of the time we could occasionally hit it to the fence, but because we were not very fast, we would be lucky to get a double. And even though I was told to hit the cut-off man, I always just threw the ball as hard as I could to try to get it back into the dirt of the infield, as if I had something to prove.

I knew things were awkward for me. Having long legs and arms and being overweight as a youngster, I was not very agile or coordinated and could not run very fast. My reaction time trying to catch a ball thrown to me at first base was not the best. My parents said that whenever I would try to round first base and then walk back, it looked like I was moon walking.

Technically, my address was Muncie, Indiana, but we lived out in the country, even outside the small town of Gaston. Because the county did not pave the roads, they were what was called "tarred and chipped." Basically, that means the road crews put hot liquid asphalt down and threw stone over the top of it to create the pavement. It was a cheaper version of straight asphalt. One day during baseball season, my mom took Kevin and me for a bike ride down our road. When I turned around to go home, my wheel caught the edge of the stone layer and my bike slid out from under me. As usual, we had to go to the ER, this time to get the rocks taken out of my knee and get stitches. It must have taken them a little longer than expected to excavate the stones, and I should have told the doctor to put more numbing medicine on the cut, because I felt every one of the ten stitches they put in my leg.

While I was healing, I missed quite a few games and hated having to watch my team play without me. At the time, it was not as much about getting a home run or even being able to score the winning run as it was about hanging out with my teammates and enjoying our time together. The day I went to the doctor to have the stitches taken out, we had a game scheduled for that night. I asked the doctor if it was okay for me to play. With some reluctance, he said yes but to please be careful. I was so excited to finally get to play with my team. We were on the main field, which we didn't get to play on often, playing under the lights at the Harrison Elementary School diamond—so it was a big deal.

In the sixth inning of a seven-inning game, I had made it to third base when the pitcher threw a pitch that got by the catcher. I took off for home. I usually slid into a base on my right side but because that was the leg with the removed stitches, I ran like a giraffe, trying to slide into home on my left side. Once the dust settled, I went back to the dugout after high-fiving my teammates, then ran to tell Mom I had slid on the opposite knee. With relief on her face, she said, "I know. I was so worried, but I saw you slide on the opposite knee." Her next words, however, were "Now be careful. I don't want to go back to the ER again tonight." I quaked at the unwritten rule in sports about not jinxing a player.

I played the final inning, and, of course, I did end up in the ER again. I wish I could say that I had slid into home again to win the game or that I had made a diving catch for the last out. But that wasn't the case. After we had won the game, I was so excited that I ran out of the dugout. Being an eager nine-year-old who more shuffled his feet than picked them up, I wasn't paying attention to the bats, which were not placed up against the fence as they should have been but were lying on the ground. Yes, I tripped over them. I immediately yanked up my pants leg and pulled back my bandages. And yes, I had ripped the wound open again.

I spent close to six years playing baseball. The thing I loved was being a part of a team and having teammates root each other on. Even if I made a mistake in the field or struck out, they were always there to pick me up.

I also liked watching the older kids play baseball. The Wes-Del High School team played some of their games at the ball diamonds near ours, and between our games, we had time to watch them play. They made it the state finals in 1990, which, at the time, was only the second time in my high school's history for any sports team at Wes-Del to make it to the state finals. Only football was exempt from the one-class system, so schools of all sizes played against each other.

To make things even more remarkable, that year, Wes-Del needed a head baseball coach for the kids even to be able to play. The school board picked Roger Seats who had played on Wes-Del's state final-four football team in the 1970s and was our head football coach that year. The unique thing about Coach Seats was that he had never played baseball, so he picked out a few of his colleagues from the area to come coach with him. Luckily, the team had spent many years playing together successfully. In the semifinal championship game, they played Bedford North Lawrence, a high school just outside of Indianapolis that was ten times the size of Wes-Del.

It was a beautiful June day at Bush Stadium, where the Indianapolis Indians played minor league ball at the time. Though we lost the championship game 9–2, each player was presented with a medal and a trophy for being in the state final game. Being able to experience earning a medal for achieving excellence, not just watching while others received one, became something that I wanted for myself one day.

Although the years that I played, my teams never got the opportunity to play for a championship, I did learn a lot about playing sports and about life. You're never going to win every game no matter how hard you try. There is always going to be one winner and one loser. Someone is going to be happy and someone is going away in tears. In one of the last games I would get the opportunity to play in in the major leagues in elementary school, we ended the season—like everyone except the champions—with a loss. Returning to the dugout, I saw one of my teammates crying to his mom and dad. I wondered, *Was he sad because he got hurt or sad that we lost the game?* Neither. I was proud to hear him tell his mom, "I don't get to play with the Beach Boys."

CHAPTER 4

MY IDENTITY AS AN ATHLETE

I WENT THROUGH MIDDLE SCHOOL as an awkward kid. I loved being in band and was decent at it. But the only reason I was in it was to get an easy grade. I had my group of friends who hung out on Sundays, and they were the only ones who got to know the real me, even though I got along with many of my classmates, no matter what they represented. I learned from my parents to never judge someone on the outside, because it's what is on the inside that matters. I was not the most popular person in my class, but I made it a point to make sure everyone knew who I was.

Middle school was a time of constant, awkward change. My closest group of friends were in my church youth group at Mt. Olive

United Methodist Church (now Mt. Olive Church), and we continued to be friends, but it all felt different. Our identities were changing. Voices changed and bodies changed—people changed. I was searching for my identity, wanting to find what kind of person I was and who I wanted to be.

With my mom being a teacher, my grades were always the most important. In middle school, I was a conservative, shy kid. I felt a lot of the time I was just a stepping stone for many of my classmates, but I also was the type of person who wanted to be friends with everyone, no matter how I was treated sometimes. I was gratefully aware I had a great support system with my parents, which I think carried me through a lot of hard times. And I drew on my friendships with the people in my church youth group.

Going into sixth grade, I wanted to play the drums, but because most of my classmates wanted to play drums, I had to go to my second choice, the alto saxophone. I used to love watching Kenny G play. You would find me during halftime of football and basketball games playing in the band. I always wanted to be the loudest so everyone could hear me—it became a competition for me. Once I got into high school, I eventually made first-chair saxophone most of the time, which I was proud of.

Up until the seventh grade, all our teachers called Kevin and me by our last name. My math teacher, Mr. Colter, was the first one to change that after he told us if we wore different clothes, he would call us by our first names. The next day we each wore a sweat suit: mine had IU on it, and Kevin's had Purdue. It fit the criteria, so we went with it. Hearing *my* name, Kurt, from a teacher was the first time I felt like my own person. I had always thought up to this point that, as a twin, you always had to do things the same.

This moment I will never forget and would reign more prominent in my life as I got older.

The one thing I enjoyed the most in middle school though, was my involvement in sports, even though I struggled with speed and jumping. I remember going into the coach's classroom the first day they made announcements about trying out for the sixth-grade basketball team. Mr. Eckelman knew my dad from working at Warner Gear, so I thought I'd go see what it was about. He told all the boys, "If you are planning on playing for me, be prepared to run." The first thing I thought—like my dad years before—was *Where is the door?* I could not wait to get out of that room, because I knew that was not something that I wanted to be told to do. I loved playing basketball in the backyard, but running was not my strong suit.

A few days later, I got interested in trying out for wrestling. For some reason, I felt like the training was not that bad. I worked hard during practices and was able to do most of the activities and moves they tried to teach us. I was probably five, eleven and 180 pounds at the time, kind of a bigger kid for a sixth grader. I did struggle with trying to get off my knees and up to a standing position with my arms behind my back. Out of the many times I tried it, only once was I able to do it successfully. Midway through the season, I felt embarrassed because I was not as strong as some of the kids and was fearful of failing—or maybe it was because I had to wear that skin-tight suit. However, I persevered through the season but didn't do wrestling as much as I was just helping with the team. One of the first matches, I was all ready to go, but I did not want to get out on the mat knowing that everyone's eyes would be watching me and knowing I was not the most athletic person on the team and might make a fool of myself by getting beat.

During my seventh- and eighth-grade years, I decided to return to basketball where I felt more comfortable. This time it was different from rec league in elementary school, although I still wasn't fast or a good jumper. My least favorite drill was "tens," where we would run down to one end of the gym and do ten wall jumps then run back to the other side and do nine, and so forth all the way down to one. During that drill, Kevin and I maybe jumped two inches up the wall with great effort. I think most of the kids were glad Kevin and I were so slow because they got a little longer break than we did. We mainly were put on the B squad and played against the kids who did not get to play in the main game. I enjoyed playing those games because we were not pressured to win and still got to play a full game. We played a lot of two to three zone defense where we didn't have to run to match up with the other team, and Kevin and I were still taller than most of the kids, so we took up a lot of space in the paint. On offense, we would do a lot of passing back and forth across the rim before we either put the ball in the basket or someone was able to sneak in between us and grab it.

Before one of our games in eighth grade, my coach came up to me and told me I was going to start in the main game. He said he was allowing me to do this because of the work I had put into the B game the week before and how much I had hustled. I was so excited that night and could not wait to see my parents at the game. Back then, we did not have cell phones for texting our parents or Snapchat or Instagram for posting our exploits. If we had that technology, you better believe me, I would have tweeted the crap out of that moment. The best part was that during warm-ups, when instead of all the starters shooting and me just passing them the ball, I got to do some shooting too. Even though it was the first time I was going to be playing in the main game, instead of hogging the ball, I let the others who normally played get plenty of warm-up also.

I knew I wasn't going to play that much, but I was still nervous and felt like a fish out of water at tip-off. I was not playing with the kids I usually played with who tried to get me the ball when they could. And I knew whenever I did get the ball passed to me, I would try to pass to the ones who played more often so they could score. I feared I would screw something up and felt the pressure of not wanting to be the one who caused our team to lose. As it turned out, I played only about two minutes.

I wish I could tell you that we won the game, but I really don't remember. And I would love to tell you that I got to start more games throughout the year, but that just wasn't the case. However, it was the first time I felt like I had accomplished something in sports, and it sparked my drive to work my way into that position again. Those two minutes gave me the confidence that if I worked hard, I would get rewarded. I was aware that the only way I felt okay with myself was as an athlete. Was I very good? No way. But being with athletes on a team and being an athlete made me feel like a real person somehow.

I was happy to enter high school and start this new chapter of more freedom as our parents finally started loosening their grip and letting us become individuals! Some say high school is the "best four years of your life." For me, it was the best educational experiences in my life and was fun because I learned not just from reading books or listening to someone teaching me geometry (which I still hate today), but through every bit of my education. It all gave me the knowledge and skills to make it through life and helped me learn who I wanted to be as an individual.

As soon as I walked through the doors of Wes-Del High School, I reverted to the insecure middle school kid. Growing up a twin, I would say ninety-five percent of the time, Kevin and I were dressed in the same outfit. My parents figured when they found good deals on clothing, why not buy two of them? One outfit we wore stands out in my memory: the one we wore at Disney World's Magic Kingdom just outside the Sea Quest area. We had the plain blue shorts hiked up above our waists to where the crease of the shorts actually bunched up slightly in the groove between our hips and groin—borderline "camel toe" but for boys. On top of that, we wore white shirts tucked into the waistband, and we had white tube socks that came midway up our shins. To top it off, we had haircuts like Jim Carrey's in *Dumb and Dumber*. Our look was styling, for sure, and reminded me of Tweedledee and Tweedledum from the 1951 Walt Disney classic *Alice in Wonderland*.

We never had the fanciest new $250 Jordan's or the designer blue jeans, but I was lucky that when I needed clothes or anything, for the most part, there was not a "no" from my parents. They worked hard for what we had, and they showed me that it's not always what you have but who you are. That didn't exactly register at the time. The first time I got a paycheck from one of the many jobs I had in high school, I bought myself my first pair of Tommy John blue jeans. I thought they were the coolest thing ever.

Sure, our high school had a pecking order like most schools. You know that obvious hierarchy you see and survival-of-the-fittest feel you get when you are a freshman in the same lunch room with the seniors? That about to get shoved into the lockers by the six-five, 280-pound lineman on the football team type of feeling? Sometimes it was like that, but our class at West-Del High School felt different than most classes. Our middle school principal at our graduation said we were the worst class to have attended there. Sharon Staley, who became a teacher my sixth-grade year, saw us differently. We were her first class, and she became close with our class and my group of friends in youth group. She told us that the reason our class seemed so tough was that we were hard to break apart. We always stuck close to one another and had each other's back even when times got rough. We never had serious fights between us, although there were some disputes among us. But we always stuck together.

I looked at everyone in my class as equals, no one better than the rest. I was always the social person who loved to talk to anyone, but never felt part of any specific group in school. I believe I got that from my dad, who never met a person he did not get to know. But I also knew that around the kids at my high school, I felt really insecure with myself and was unable to let people truly see who I was on the inside because of my insecurities on the outside.

My first high school gym class was with Mr. Howell. He knew my brother and me because we had done track for three years as throwers in middle school. After the bell rang that first day, Mr. Howell stopped Kevin and me and asked if we wanted to be managers for the cross-country team. Of course, being the son of my mother, who could not say no to anyone who asked her to do anything, Kevin and I both said we would help out. I went to every practice and every meet they had. I helped them clean the trail back in the woods and timed the mile splits at the meets. I was also in charge of Coach's stuff at the meets. At one meet, the Rushville Cross-Country Invitational, it was a cold morning, so I wore a jacket. After getting to the meet, Coach Howell gave me the keys to the only van we had taken to the meet, so he didn't lose them on the course while he was running around. My parents, being supportive, went to all the meets too. Later while we were waiting for the meet results to come up, my parents decided to take off. Since the sun had come out from behind the morning clouds and it had gotten warmer throughout the day, I gave them my jacket to take home.

After the meet, we packed up all of the stuff and were ready to leave. Coach came over and asked for the van keys. I immediately reached for my jacket pocket then stopped short as I realized they and my jacket were in my parents' car, which had just left twenty-five minutes earlier. I thought, *what were we going to do?* And Coach was going to kill me. I raised my hands with a shiver in my voice and said, "Coach, um, I had them in my coat and my parents took it in their car." He said nothing, but we found a school phone and left a message at my home for my parents to call us when they got home. We were about ninety minutes away from home, so we all knew it was going to be a while. As much as that situation sucked to be stuck there for that long, we bonded as a team while we waited, and even though I was the culprit for keeping everyone there, I actually became part of the group that day.

Even after that incident, Coach Howell let me come back year after year. I loved to hang around them because, even though I was the manager, I felt like I was part of the team. We all loved hanging out at the meets, except for some of the really cold and rainy ones when no one wanted to be there. My senior year, Coach Howell gave Kevin and me our four-year award for cross-country and thanked us for the dedication we gave him all those years.

After my freshman year of cross-country, Kevin and I began freshman basketball. Somehow after middle school, many of the kids in my class became more muscular and way faster. While a lot of them had been training during the summer, I did not love extra conditioning or being in the weight room. Instead I spent most of my summer months working as a corn detasseler. This is a common Iowa process. When corn is planted, four female rows are planted with one male row in between. To create hybridized field corn, we detasselers took the tassel off the female stalks so they would not become pollinated by the males. Detasseling is hot work and basically involves a lot of walking and sweating. So going into that freshman season, I was not in the greatest shape compared to my fellow classmates.

I also knew I was going to be put on the B team again. Halfway through the season, I developed some knee pain after running. I went to an orthopedic doctor and was diagnosed with patellofemoral syndrome, sometimes called "runner's knee." Through some physical therapy to relieve the pain around my kneecaps, the therapists noticed that my quadriceps were not as strong as my hamstrings, so they began trying to strengthen them. After that season, even though I enjoyed playing the game, I figured I was done for high school basketball because I was not going to be good enough to be a JV player and there were no more B teams.

That next fall in my sophomore year, because I knew I was not getting strong enough to compete in track and field, I began to play on our high school golf team. My grandfather used to love to take Kevin and me to this local par-three course while my mom and grandmother played a round of miniature golf. My first two years on the team, our coach was not present often. He would show up most of the time at practice but just play a round with a few of the groups and try to teach us as we played. Often we would find ourselves at the course by ourselves, just hoping he would show up for our matches.

It wasn't until my senior year that my competitiveness on the golf course finally emerged. That year we had a new coach, Coach Walters, who had been my eighth-grade basketball coach. The first four weeks of practice we never touched foot on the course unless we wanted to after practice. We would each get a bucket of balls and set up on the driving range. After everyone was done hitting their bucketful, we would have to walk out onto the range and pick up enough balls to fill our buckets. We would do that four or five times a day.

After the first week, I had calluses on my hands from hitting all those balls. But by that first meet, wow, what a difference. The previous two years, the lowest most of us scored was around double-bogie, which is about eighteen strokes over par. My senior year, though, most of us were down to around a bogie golf score, nine strokes over par. Once coach noticed how much better we were, he made a bet with most of the team. The average par score for nine holes was between thirty-four and thirty-six depending on the course. As a team, you took the total lowest scores of your top five golfers then threw out the highest score of those five. He bet us if we could score a total of 180 strokes in a match, which would be about forty-five strokes for each golfer, he would buy the starting five golfers steak dinners. So that year, we had two goals to shoot for—steak and to maybe win a match, which we had never done.

We came really close in many of our matches to breaking that 180 score. In one of my matches, I scored a forty-three (par was thirty-five), a personal best. After the match, I came home so excited to tell my mom, that as I came in, I shut my thumb in the front door. That night my thumb swelled and started to turn black and blue. I woke up in the middle of the night with the worst throbbing in my thumb I have ever felt.

What do you do when you're a Beach? Do you go to the hospital to have them look at it? No. Your dad makes a needle out of a safety pin, lights up the end with his lighter so it's hot enough to sterilize it, then pierces three holes in your nail bed to relieve the pressure. Although the piercing hurt just as bad as the throbbing, releasing the blood behind my nail bed was the worst. For the next nine days, I was restricted to putting on the green since I could not grip my club.

While on the green, I noticed a petite, under-five-foot girl who came up to our group. She was waiting for her brother who was playing on a team we shared our course with. Her name was Delana, and she was a cheerleader and golfer for a school's team up the road near where I lived. We began talking and eventually started dating. So that was the silver lining from my smashed thumb—the something good that came out of a setback.

When Delana and I started to date, my focus changed. Though we were complete opposites, that connection I wanted was there with her. However, sports were still on my mind, at least some of the time, according to Coach Walters. One night after a match, the top four golfers were told to stay behind after everyone left because none of us had shot well in the match. I had told Coach that I always played better with Jared Niccum, and Kevin always played well with Jeremy Fisher, so that match he had switched us up, but we all shot about what we had two years before and nowhere close to what we had been averaging that year. After the match, Coach was fired up at us and yelled at us unlike anything I'd experienced. He screamed at me, "You are more worried about a girl than you are about golf. If you just want to be average and not focus, then go ahead. We can finish the season back where you had the previous years." That hit me right in the gut.

After Coach left, the four of us talked. First, we laughed because we were so shocked we had been yelled at for our golf scores. But then we agreed it was something we had been wanting for a few years—a coach who cared. His yelling was his way of showing he cared about us and about our accomplishing the goals we had set. We decided if we refocused on the goal, we could achieve whatever we wanted. That year our team did better than we had in the previous five years, and I learned a valuable lesson about prioritizing and cultivating a desire for improvement.

My sophomore through senior years, I also was the manager for the basketball team. I would help Coach Moffett every day after school, setting up for practices and helping on game days. I also helped run the summer leagues by taking stats and running the scoreboards. We had a ton of great basketball games, and I was able to see the best athletes from all the schools in Delaware County come out to play. Two were well-known players from Muncie Central, Steve Smith and Bonzi Wells, who were both recruited and signed to play at Ball State after graduation.

As manager, I also helped tape some of the players' ankles before practice. From dealing with some of my own aches and pains, I began to take notice of the athletic trainer, Mary Jacobs, who came to our school. She taught Kevin and me some of the skills and knowledge she had about athletic training. It was after working with Mary for two years that I knew what I wanted to do. I loved sports and being around sports, and I knew I wanted to be an athletic trainer. Though I was never going to be any type of athlete other than recreational, I wanted to help others be able to participate and excel at whatever sport they loved.

CHAPTER 5

AFTER THE DIAGNOSIS: MY FINDING HOPE

JUST WHEN THE PICTURE OF WHO I WAS and what I wanted to do with my life was clearing, present-day life clouded over with the diagnosis of SMA (spinal muscular atrophy) and the neurologist's dire prediction that summer before college. In the weeks after my diagnosis, I did a lot of thinking about what I was going to do, most of the time in silence. My roller-coaster life was hurtling downward out of control. Mom didn't know what to say other than to tell people to pray for us. Many people apologized to us that we all had to go through such a thing. I thought, *why are they apologizing? It is what it is, and I just need to figure out what I am supposed to do.* Kevin was dealing with his similar diagnosis in his own way, so I didn't even feel we could talk. I had my friends, family, and people I went to church with, but still felt so alone, with no guidance or structure in my life. On top of that, I was embarrassed and didn't want to broadcast my condition to many people.

I felt like I had leprosy (known today as Hansen's disease), which I'd read about in the Bible, where it appears sixty-eight times (fifty-five in the Old Testament and thirteen times in the New Testament). In biblical times, it was thought this disfiguring, infectious disease originated from sin and was a curse from God put upon individuals as a punishment. The condition ruins the nerves, preventing individuals from feeling sensations, including pain from extreme heat or in individuals with diabetes, the decay of their own feet. People with leprosy generally were looked at as being unclean or dirty and were shunned. I knew I didn't look like those who were ravaged with the disease and I wasn't shunned as unclean and deserving of divine punishment, but I did feel separate from others and didn't want people to think less of me or tease or pity me because of my condition. I was afraid and in one fell swoop had lost my growing certainty of my identity. My vision of who I was and my future was dimmed and shaky, and I started searching all over again.

I knew I had to create a new focus, but what would that look like? Where was I going to go from here? I didn't know. There was a lot of doubt in my head about what I should or could do. I knew I had to do something though; I couldn't just stay strapped in the roller-coaster seat paralyzed and at the whim of the ride. So I started doing a lot of biking because I loved being outside and moving my body with purpose. Outside, alone, was when I could do my best thinking. Biking through the countryside with an occasional car passing by gave me a lot of opportunity to think and do some soul searching—and even some crying. I prayed to God a lot, asking him, "Why is this happening to me? What am supposed to do now? If I go the route that I want to, am I going to be able to make it? Will I be confined to a wheelchair? And if so, when? What do I need to do to make this better?" I even begged. "Can you just take this away, please?" I had many questions but not very many answers.

One night I was riding, I remembered the song "Unanswered Prayers" by Garth Brooks, which is about being grateful for unanswered prayers because they don't mean God doesn't care, and they can be his greatest gifts. And I thought to myself, *there must be a reason why God put me on this earth and why this was happening to me*. And I knew he would reveal that to me when ready. As this thought strengthened into a belief over time and with continued prayer, I came to some peace with the diagnosis and knew that if I just trusted in God, he would show me what I needed to do.

One Sunday morning in church, after the message, I had this feeling that God wanted me to turn my life over to him. This verse from Isaiah had stuck with me since my youth group meetings: "So do not fear, for I am with you; do not be dismayed, for I am your god. I will strengthen you and help you; I will uphold you with my righteous right hand." (Isaiah 41:10 NLT) Sitting in church that day, I knew it was time for me to recognize I could not do this myself, and I was not alone. It was time to have God lead me and for me to follow him without restraint.

I leaned on other Bible stories too. Like the one from Luke 6:6–10 about another Sabbath, when Jesus entered the synagogue and was teaching and a man was there whose right hand was withered. The scribes and the Pharisees watched Jesus to see whether he would heal on the Sabbath, which was against their laws. They wanted to find a reason to accuse him. But Jesus knew their thoughts, and he said to the man, "Come and stand here." And the man rose and stood there. Jesus said to them, "I ask you, is it lawful on the Sabbath to do well or to do harm, to save life or to destroy it?" And after looking around at them, he said to the man, "Stretch out your hand." He did so, and his hand was restored. Jesus was here to bring people to God, and he showed the man this by reaching out his hand as an invitation to follow him. God would heal his wounds if he just received it. Unlike that man, I knew that I was not going to be instantly healed, but like him, I needed to be a follower. At that moment, Jesus was reaching out his hand to me. I accepted, and a few weeks later I was baptized.

In my Methodist church, they did not do many full-body immersion baptisms. The only time it usually was done was during our church picnic at the end of summer, down at the house of one of the church members, less than five hundred yards from where I grew up. They had a huge pond where all the kids used to swim and dive off the diving board, while all the adults sat back and ate each other's potluck dishes. I remember there was always just enough food to feed all of us and plenty of desserts. Many times at those events, people who had turned themselves over to Christ got baptized. The picnic had already passed the year I wanted to be baptized, so the pastor did a sprinkling of water over my forehead. Kevin and I both were baptized in this way.

After that day, I had some clarity and hope. To say I did not still have some doubt and fear would be lying, but I knew I just had to have faith and keep searching for purpose. I also knew that in order for me to keep what health I had, I needed to begin to lose some weight and gain as much strength as I could. Off to the weight room

I went. During high school I was not much of a weight room type of guy, especially in public, because I knew I wasn't very strong. But this time it was different. I had an urgent purpose for being there and it gave me drive. I would go in and just do whatever I felt like doing that day with no direction. I still did not want to feel judged by other people, and I did not want anyone to know about my condition. But I couldn't help but see all of the big guys putting so much weight on the bars or curling these massive dumbbells.

I chose weight machines that had pictures on them so I could see what muscles I was working on and could switch the weight to make it easier or harder for me. I also chose those where plates could be added or subtracted to fit me. I also liked that the back of the machine usually was covered by the plates so no one knew what weight I was lifting. As a young man, image was so important to me. Before leaving the machine, I would move the pin three or four holes higher in the stack so the person who used it next would think I had lifted more weight than I actually had. With all my tricks and comparing myself to others, it never really sank in how much weaker I was than my peers.

My career was another big piece of my life I needed to figure out as part of my healing. I called our curriculum director in the Ball State athletic training program, Dr. Michael Ferrara, a few weeks after my neurology appointment to seek guidance on what I should do. I told him if he could give me some direction that would give me some sort of hope that being an athletic trainer was what I could do for the rest of my life. He said, "Kurt, do what you feel you were called to do in life. If it is being an athletic trainer, then put one hundred percent of your effort into it." That was just what I needed to hear, and I'll always be grateful for Dr. Ferrara's encouragement.

They say, on average, a third of college students change their major at least once with in their first three years, and one out of ten changes it more than once. But I knew that I wanted to be able to work with athletes and help them get back to playing sports. My fears, however, still made me wonder if that truly was what I was meant to do. Worse, they made me question how it was going to work if my body was not going to stand up to the rigors of the profession. I did have one answer for myself—being an athletic trainer was the only thing I knew I wanted to do. And my faith held the thought for me that God was working on my body and my soul, and he was going to give me the knowledge and determination to get me through college with whatever career would give me the most joy in my life. I just had to keep showing up, searching for him and that joy and purpose.

CHAPTER 6

COLLEGE AND FIRST STEPS IN ATHLETIC TRAINING

AFTER THE DIAGNOSIS, I began leaning on the insights and qualities I had cultivated playing sports, starting with taking inventory of my inner strengths. I saw persistence as one of them. How many times did I practice shooting a free throw before I could do it without bricking it off the backboard or not even hitting the rim? How many times did I work on putting the ball in the hole on the golf course, instead of pushing it far past the hole or shooting it nowhere near the hole? And how long did I practice at it to get to where I needed only to two-putt it in instead of taking three or four strokes? So, I identified I could draw on my persistence now.

Then there was patience. I had waited for such a long time to be able to get in even one A team game in middle school. But I was given that opportunity one day because I was determined and had a great attitude while being patient until I earned that spot. Commitment came to me as I remembered getting yelled at by my golf coach because I lost my focus, then recovered it with renewed dedication. From that point, I trained myself to focus on my goal, even though in the back of my mind I had this diagnosis hovering over me. I was committed to becoming an athletic trainer above all, so I was able to shift my focus to the positive or call on God to help.

Getting into athletic training was harder than it had appeared in high school. Seeing the different aspects of what made a successful sports medicine team was fascinating but complex. Of course, you have the athlete first and foremost. You have the first responders or whoever needs to get the athlete to the hospital. And you have the doctor who orders all the necessary tests and who has the expertise to make a diagnosis. And the doctors have their people who take care of getting things ready for any surgery. The physical therapist comes in to help with the athlete's rehabilitation, as well as the nutritionist who takes care of the athlete's bodily needs to regain top physical condition. And you have the strength coaches who push the athletes to increase their strength and endurance. Finally, the coach is there to make the game plan and keep the athlete motivated to win that next competition.

Guess who is right in the center of them all, restoring the health and confidence of the athlete and making sure they are ready for that next game? Yep, the athletic trainer. I loved being the person behind the scenes who made it possible for the athletes to stay in the game and try to give their team the chance to win. Just as in high school as the manager for the teams, I was always there to help with the little things at practice to make everything go smoothly and flawlessly throughout the competitions so the athletes could be at their best. Being an athletic trainer was a combination of multiple disciplines. I am on the field when an injury occurs, reacting as a first responder. I also am there as a kind of physician to determine the extent of the injury and help make a plan for rehabbing and implementing it. Best of all, I'm there as a motivator and supporter for the athlete as they eventually return to the sport they so much enjoy.

My first semester at Ball State went by in a blur, and Kevin and I approached college differently. School was the most important thing, but I also liked to have fun. I was no party animal, but I enjoyed being around people, especially athletes. I went to parties I was invited to just to hang out, not to drink. To this day, I have never touched alcohol or drugs or even smoked a cigarette. My dad was a smoker until I was twelve, and I was not going to begin something like that and not be able to quit, so I avoided it. I also enjoyed my sleep when it came to bedtime. Studying the night before an exam was extremely important to me, but getting some sleep was equally important. I went to bed around midnight and liked to get up the morning of an exam around seven to study more. Kevin, on the other hand, would go to bed around two or three then get up around six a.m.

As an entry-level athletic training student, I had to log time observing and helping with teams in addition to adjusting to college life and classwork. I spent as much time as I could either down in the training room at Worthen Arena or out on the basketball courts or over at the baseball diamonds. I was showing the staff members and the faculty of the program how dedicated I was to doing this. To make ends meet, I also was working at the Finish Line athletic shoe store in the Muncie mall. At first, I was the shy kid who did not know what he was doing, but with some great mentors, who were also college students and in the same boat, I learned the ropes and transformed from the guy who was afraid to go up to anyone and ask them if they needed help to, by the end of that first year, overseeing the entire kids' and women's shoe departments and being the one people asked for when they came in to be fitted for the proper shoe.

My bosses saw my drive to always achieve more. At Finish Line, unlike many other athletic shoe companies, we didn't work on commission. However, they would give us a sales goal, depending on the number of hours we worked on the floor, something called a multiple sales ratio. This meant, for everything I sold, I should encourage add-ons to go with the primary sale. Say I sold a pair of shoes. I would also try to sell either a pair of socks, shoe orthotics, cleaners, or maybe a jogging sweatshirt. The more multiple sales per transaction I made, the higher my multiple sales ratio. My goal every night was not just to beat that ratio but to crush it. In my time working there, there were more times that I beat it than I fell short of it. That was my competitive spirit at work.

Toward the end of that first year, I had worked my way into position to apply to the athletic training program at Ball State. In order to be accepted, I needed to demonstrate worthiness through my observation hours and schoolwork. I worked my butt off to boost my GPA, and I don't remember any C's except for maybe two general education courses. Reference letters also were a big part of the application. Kay Saunders was the athletic director for Wes-Del High School and a longtime friend to my brother and me when we were students. Kevin and I had frequently helped her set up the gyms for sports events and anything else she needed. Our senior year,

Kay gave us both her service award as a sign of thanks for our hard work. Kay was always my biggest supporter so, of course, hers was the first reference letter I had. If I passed the first hurdle, the staff and education faculty would interview me to determine if I would be the right fit. My brother and I were both grateful to get interviews.

This interview was probably the most important one of my life. It was the culmination of the past year of overcoming heartache to see if I could do what I felt called to do. I wore my one pair of old dress pants, a shirt, tie, and sports jacket, and sat outside the room, nervous, with my brother next to me. Some of the people knew about my condition, but I was afraid I would be judged and told again that I should probably get a desk job. I don't remember any of the questions they asked me, and coming out of that interview, I was not sure either of us would be accepted. So we waited. A few days later, it was announced there were only two spots available, and only one person from my class got in. And that one person was not me or Kevin.

I was extremely disappointed, but I was not going to let it get me down. I was reminded of the times at home running off raccoons from our house and backing them into a corner with nowhere to go. I have never seen a raccoon in that situation curl up in a ball in the fetal position pretending it was dead; they do not play possum. Nope, they stand up as big as they can get, arms out, claws out, and teeth showing they're ready to fight. That's how I felt, and that was fueled even more that evening when I told my mom the news. She said, "The good thing is you know what they are going to ask in the interviews now so you can prepare for next time. All you need to do is to put more time in to show them you really want this." I have never forgotten those words from my mother that day. It's like the proverb that says you may get knocked down seven times but what counts is getting up the eighth time.

educational coordinators I had gotten to know very well over the semester because she had taught our lab on taping, was one of the interviewers in my room. The room itself was dim and dreary with an oval table the interviewers sat behind and one open chair in the middle for me to sit in. I really wanted to stand in case I needed to run. I felt like a deer in the woods that saw some pellets lying on the ground. They would eat them while standing, fearing the whole time they might need to escape quickly. Yep, I was in flight or fight mode—or what my dad called "scared shitless."

But I decided to sit. I left my sports coat on because I already was sweating and did not want to show stains on my shirt. Connie said, "Now take a deep breath, Kurt. This isn't your first go-round." I gently smiled and took a large, deep breath. I wish it would totally have calmed my nerves, but it didn't. What was on the line in this interview was too big. It was going to be my next step in completing my career, and in the back of my mind, in proving my neurologist wrong.

The first questions were typical ones: What made you want to be an athletic trainer? What have you learned about athletic training so far? Everything was going smoothly, and I began to get comfortable and relax. Then Rex Stump, the head athletic trainer of the program as well as for the football team, asked his first question. In my observation time of the football teams, I did not get to know Stump very well. The only thing the students in the program told me about him was to just do what he said and not ask questions. So I was intimidated at his blunt question: "I see you currently have a C minus in your lower extremity class. In our program, you will be working an average of at least thirty-five hours a week with teams. How are you going to balance your schoolwork and ATC hours?" Despite my fear, I could see where he was going and explained, "We have had only one big exam and one practical exam. I got an A on the practical one but did not fare as well on the regular exam." I took a breath and told him most of the kids in my class got low grades on that exam. I continued, "I understand how that grade looks, but if you look at the rest of my grades in my prerequisite classes, I have gotten all A's and only two C's. Plus, when I was in high school, I was seventh in my class with a 3.55 grade point average." I concluded by saying I had adjusted my studying patterns since that exam and was sure I had done much better on yesterday's exam and promised him I was bringing that grade up.

His next question was a kick to the right side of my chest, an uppercut to the lower jaw, then a kick right to the balls. Yep, I said it. He said, "I see that you and your brother are both applying again to the program. If your brother gets into the program and you don't, what will you do next?" I kind of took a few seconds to recover and think about that. I had been through so much in my life already and had finally come into a little bit of peace about my life and what it looked like. But being an athletic trainer was a huge part of it. I took a deep breath and said in the most honest way I could, "I will keep trying until I am accepted. So I guess I would apply again next semester. I have wanted to do this since I was a junior in high school." That was it. I was done, I thought to myself as I left the room. Then I figured they had already picked who they wanted because Kevin said he didn't get that question. The list of who had been accepted would be posted on the door at the ATC Lab by nine a.m. two days from then.

That night, I rolled over and over in my head all the questions they had asked and how I answered them. Did I say the right thing? Could I have said anything different that would have made me look any better than the other individuals applying? I kept rehashing my references too. I wondered if they had even called my references. I tried to take hope from what Kay Saunders had said when Kevin and I asked her to be a reference for the second time. She told us, "This is going to be the one for a Beach Boys' victory. I just know it." It helped, but I could still barely sleep the next two nights.

That second morning arrived, and I did not have a class until ten that day, so Kevin and I rushed at 8:30 to the ATC Lab on the second floor of the Human Performance Building. We sat on the floor with five other people in my class waiting for the results. We all talked about the questions we were asked during our interviews. I mentioned that they asked me what I would do if I did not get in and Kevin did. The others said they thought they would soil themselves if they were asked that. It was good to have a great laugh together. Then Connie Peterson came out with the infamous white paper and a piece of tape and stuck our futures to the outside wall of the lab.

You know that scene in cheerleading movies where they post who made the squad and all the cheerleaders rush the board? That was mostly everybody who was there at that time. But I slowly got myself off the floor and waited until my classmates and Kevin scoured the list and celebrated. I was the last one to make it up to the list, for fear of others seeing the disappointment in my face when I didn't see my name on the list. As I scrolled down the list with my finger, I came across the listing: "Spring Football Kurt Beach." I had made it! Something I had waited for, which seemed out of reach for so long, was finally here. Now it was time to go to work.

CHAPTER 7

MY FIRST TEAMS AND CAMP WOODWARD

MY LIFE DREAM WAS STARTING to become a reality, and I was living my life without regrets, not even about giving up playing some of the sports I loved so I would not get hurt and have a setback. I had studied hard, become more outgoing, and had made it to the point where I thought if I went no further, at least I knew I had tried. But new doubts arose: Will I fit in with the teams I'm helping or will I be judged for my disability? Will I exceed my expectations? I have showed grit and determination, but will I keep living up to that? And an old question remained: Will I succeed? All I knew for sure at that point was it was time to put up or shut up on this stage of my journey.

I had renewed drive after getting into the program. My life was lived in the gym working out six days a week to make myself as strong as I could be in order to fight my condition. Now it was time to buckle down, learn all I could, and graduate, all while getting the most out of life.

My first assignment was with spring football. It was such a weird feeling being behind the learning curve and scrambling to get up to speed with all the athletes going through rehab. But it was great to finally be able to do more than just observe. That semester flew by. Getting to know the football players—and them getting to know me—took some time. I was the sole person in charge at open work-outs at the stadium, but I also had support from an older student in the program. I learned a lot and gained confidence, as I was finally able to use some of the skills I had learned in classes. The student athletes treated me as one of their own, and I fit in just fine. It was an amazing feeling to be wanted by the athletes and to be able to help them.

My next assignment came out a few weeks before the end of the semester—women's swimming and diving. My first reaction, I'm chagrined to admit, was disappointment because I was afraid the work wouldn't be challenging. I had just finished with football, and even though it was spring ball, it was still football.

But that semester, I learned never to judge by appearances, as I came to love working with this atypical sport, and it was probably the closest I felt with any of the teams I worked with at Ball State. Yes, many times I caught myself dozing off due to the constant wave action and how warm it was in the pool, but the athletes took me in as family. One night the team had a sleepover at a campground, and they wanted me to come over for dinner. They made my dinner for me and were so excited I was there. They never treated me as their athletic trainer, which obviously was what I was there to do; they acted more like I was a teammate.

It was funny that the only way I could recognize the girls out of the pool was if they pulled their hair back and put a hand on their foreheads to mimic the caps they wore in the water. Throughout that year traveling with the team, I got to know many of them well. And I got a life's worth of lessons about females in just a few months. That they were comfortable talking about that stuff while I was in the van was pretty amazing.

We had a girl on the team that year, Elizabeth (Beth) Scott who was one of our butterflies. This young lady was the only athlete in all the sports I covered who could actually tell my twin brother and me apart. And she could tell because she could hear, not see, the difference between us. Beth was legally blind and could see only shadow images of whoever was standing in front of her, but she could hear and recognize anyone by their voice. Beth was a member of the 1996 Women's Paralympic Team in Atlanta and won a few medals there. The thing I loved most about her was the fact that she never let her disability bring her down. Even though this sounds scary, Beth actually rode a bike to her classes, although not at night. The joy she had for life was contagious, and you would never know she struggled with blindness because she never used it as an excuse.

She was an inspiration to me in dealing with my condition because she was able to show the people around her that she was not allowing her disability to hold her back. In fact, she made everyone not only get to know her but also love her for her personality, not her condition. At that time in my life, I felt like I was either still trying to cope with the fact of my disability, trying to not think of myself as having a disability, or flat-out denying that I even had anything wrong. Beth showed me what my life could look like living with purpose despite a disability.

My favorite moment in the program came the semester I was working with the baseball team. The swimming girls had invited me to go with them up to the MAC Championships at Eastern Michigan. The baseball team was on a road weekend, so I decided to drive up to the tournament on my own. The girls loved it, and after the meet, I pulled my car around to follow the bus back to Ball State. As I pulled up, one of the parents I had gotten to know well while I was working with the team came over. I rolled down my window and he told me, "Thanks so much for coming up here. The girls loved that you were able to make it up. Here is a little something to help you with your gas." As I reached out my hand, he handed me a twenty dollar bill. My instant reaction was, "No, you don't have to do that," and I started to hand it back to him. He put his hand on mine and rolled my hand closed then said, "It meant more for the girls to see you come up here. Just take it. All the families put in a few dollars each because they knew you drove up here on your own. So take it as a thank you."

I was hooked on gratitude and knew at that moment that this was the career I was meant to have. Athletic trainers are seen in some people's eyes as the "bad" people; there to tell you that you can't play in a game or can't go to practice. But in truth, we are there to make sure all the athletes can perform at their peak and don't hurt themselves to the point they need surgery or sustain career-ending or debilitating injuries. At that moment, sitting in my car waiting on the swimming team to head home, supporting the team just by my presence and being thanked for it, I knew I was in the place I needed to be.

By the end of my junior year, I had seen a plethora of injuries, but I was wanting more observation time, so I picked up extra events to cover, not only for the experience but also to get paid. I remember working at the high school Hoosier State Games one summer where I got the opportunity to work soccer and lacrosse.

On the first night of the games, I was covering lacrosse and had an injured athlete approach me to take a look at his wrist. Nervous as can be, sitting next to three people who were certified ATs (athletic trainers), I completed my evaluation. A certified AT also needed to take a look at the individual, since they were more experienced. So after I was done, I looked at one of the guys standing next to me and told him I was a student and asked if he would look at the injury also. He gave me a shocked look and said, "Oh, I didn't know you were just a student; you did a better job at looking at that than I would have." Talk about a confidence boost.

On the last day of the games, we had a torrential downpour. The water had saturated the fields so much that about eighty percent of the field was covered in water. Every time the ball was kicked, it would go no more than a foot ahead of the person because the water was so high on the field. At one of the last games, while I was sitting in a golf cart with no roof getting soaked, the goalie ran out from the goal and slid trying to scoop the ball up. At the same time, the guy on offense was approaching the ball to kick it. They got to the ball at the same time and slid so far, the offensive guy missed the ball but accidentally kicked the goalie in the mouth. It was good the goalie had braces because without them, most of his teeth would have been knocked out—although I'm sure the braces added to his pain. I was glad there was a certified AT there who knew more about what to do. I became interested in trauma after that event and realized I needed to get more experience with those types of injuries.

Toward the end of my junior year, I got to talking to another student, Jamie Oetzel, about her experiences at a camp she worked at the summer before in Pennsylvania called Camp Woodward. She spoke about all the types of injuries she saw and was able to take care of. Jamie used to be a Level 10 gymnast at Cincinnati Gymnastics, one of the most elite gyms in the country. Jamie had received a letter from Arizona State University and was possibly on her way to competing in Division I gymnastics before she blew out her patella tendon in one knee and decided to hang up her grips. She came to Ball State to become an athletic trainer and do cheerleading. Jamie had gone to Woodward as a camper in grade school and decided the year after she was accepted to the program to apply to be one of the athletic trainers on staff there. Jamie told me she was not going to go again, so I asked her if she would put in a good word for me if I applied. She said absolutely yes.

I applied in early January because Jamie said they fill up pretty quickly. I waited most of that spring without hearing anything and almost gave up. But finally I got a call one day from an unknown number. It was Gary Ream, one of the owners of Camp Woodward. He asked me about my experiences as a student and what my availability was for the summer. After a few minutes of talking, he asked if I would want to come to Camp Woodward the next week and start work. My jaw dropped, then I immediately said yes.

Seven days later, I was headed to Woodward, Pennsylvania, for a summer of learning as much as could. Pulling up to camp, my first thought was, *How far out in the middle of Amish country is this place?* My second was, *How enormous is this place?* The Disneyland of extreme sports and gymnastics sat on eighty acres amid rolling mountains of central Pennsylvania. The first two days before the camp started, I tried to get oriented to where all the skate buildings and the areas for cheerleading and gymnastics were. I met the rest of the athletic training staff the first day of camp. There were two certified trainers there besides me. They told me I would oversee everything that came in, and if I was busy or needed any help, they would be right there to assist.

The first week of camp, I was excited to see injuries start to come in. I know what you're thinking—what a sick mind. But when your job is to deal with injuries, they're what you need so you can put your schoolwork to good use and be helpful. And being of service was what I was really excited for, not the injuries themselves. The first day we responded to a skateboarder who had injured his wrist. When we got to the kid, it was obvious his wrist was broken. I had no clue what needed to be done. We took the splints we had on hand, and I assisted the certified AT with me with the splinting. We were in a remote location with the nearest hospital forty-five minutes away at State College (home of the Penn State Nittany Lions), and the nearest volunteer fire/ambulance crew was twenty minutes away. So if we could splint an injury, we could put them in a car and get them to the ER quicker than calling for an ambulance. Over the next several weeks the more injuries we had, the more confident I became, and by week three, I was doing most of the treatment for them by myself with ease.

That summer we averaged about twenty-five fractures a week. Considering there were more than nine hundred campers and three hundred fifty staff members in any given week, this was not a lot. But we were kept busy, and I got to see some of the best athletes in the world, including Amanda Borden ('96 Olympic gold medal gymnast), Andy Macdonald (pro skateboarder), Jay Miron (pro BMX), Tony Hawk (legendary X Games gold medal skateboard vert rider), and the legendary Dave Mirra (BMX rider and winner of the third most medals in X Games history).

One night of that summer I will never forget. Most of the certified people left around eight at night, but skateboarders, BMXers, and inline skaters continued to go until eleven. I got a call to the dirt jump area to evaluate one of the pro skateboarders, Brian Howard, who wanted to try out BMX dirt jumping, which are eight-foot-tall dirt jumps on a BMX bike. Brian had gone up too high on one run and was not going to safely make the down slope on the other side of the jump. Most experienced riders know when that situation occurs to throw their bike away from them before coming down on the back side of the down ramp. Brian, being a novice, held onto his bike and hit the front part of it as he fell, shoving his handlebars into the right side of his chest just below his ribs.

When I got to Brian, he complained of the area that got hit and of referred pain to his right shoulder. He also had a highly rigid stomach. Fortunately, I had just taken upper extremity evaluation the semester before, so most of the relevant information was somewhat fresh. However, I'm not going to lie, I forgot which side the liver and spleen were on. In the back of my mind, it didn't matter, because if you injured either one, it was an emergency. Plus, referred pain to the right shoulder either meant a heart attack or internal damage.

I told Brian he needed to go to the ER right away, but he was reluctant and said he thought it might just be a fractured rib. I remembered we had an ER physician visiting camp that day, so I called our nurse to see if he was still there and have him meet us at my office, which was the training room, and have a car ready to take Brian to the hospital.

After the physician evaluated him for two minutes, he told Brian he was going to the ER. He walked Brian to the car outside my office and put him in his seat. He told the driver, "Drive as fast and safely as you can. If you have to run red lights, do so at caution, but do not stop." Later we found out that Brian had lacerated his liver, and twenty minutes after arriving at the ER, he was rushed to surgery. I was so relieved I had been able to catch the signs that forced me to insist he get looked at.

Brian came back to camp after five days in the hospital, and I saw him in the shade by the pool looking like he'd been in a fight. He was physically exhausted and had a drainage pump coming from his stomach to collect excess fluid. I went over to him and asked him how he was doing. He said he was really sore and in pain, but the doctor told him he would be able to go back to skating in about six to seven weeks. Brian thanked me for being so adamant and making him go to the ER. He told me if I hadn't, he might have died. He was so appreciative of what I had done, and I felt again that I was in the right place doing what I was meant to do.

Another important lesson I learned also came from a staff member. At first I did not know what to think of Nate Wessel. He was in his twenties, six feet two, medium stature, with a scruffy beard, plus he wore scraggly jeans and T-shirts with holes, and always looked like he'd been rolling in dirt. On top of that, he had dreadlocks that went down to the middle of his back. The more I learned about Nate, however, the stereotype of a punk extreme rider dissolved. Nate lived in Pennsylvania and was the son of a carpenter who inspired Nate to do the same. He was known as a crazy shredder on a BMX bike. He would find the most unconventional path on his bike and ride it as hard and fast as he could, also trying to cover the most distance when he was in the air.

Nate was also a builder and an instructor at Camp Woodward. He loved teaching kids and creating his art of ramp building. Nate made his name by designing and building Chenga World near Cleveland while in college. The skate park eventually made it to the top spot in a rider poll of the best skate parks in the country. Eventually that landed him the position at Woodward, jobs erecting stuff for Travis Pastrana and Nitro Circus, and gigs building skate parks and vert ramps for the X Games.

I learned that the building of those parks was just as much an art as riding was. I used to see kids riding out in neighborhoods, and I thought they were there to destroy the concrete or the objects they were riding on. But getting to know Nate and the kids at Woodward, I saw all they were doing was creating art—just in a different form. It would be like trying to tell Van Gogh that how he painted was easy, when it's not. Nate did struggle with inner demons all his life and went through some hard things, but riding his bike and building amazing skate parks were productive outlets he used to clear his mind. We all have our issues in life, and some show up on the outside and some are on the inside, and we should never judge others on appearances. I would not realize till later in my life that Nate was very similar to me.

That summer was the first time in the two years after my diagnosis of spinal muscular atrophy that I forgot I had received that diagnosis because no one knew me as the guy with a disability; they knew and liked me as an athletic trainer. I still hid some aspects of my condition. For example, I used the weight room, which was near where staff members worked, when I knew no one would be there. In the lunch room, I sat on the long benches in a way that left space away from people, so I could straddle the bench and push with my hands between my legs in order to stand up. That way, neither the staff nor the kids would notice me.

One thing I loved while I was out in Pennsylvania was being able to go for a bike ride in the rolling hills of the countryside. Not only did it give me a great workout, but it was also where I first learned that riding was a time that cleared my mind and made me think a lot about what I was doing and where I was going. I knew I wasn't fully being myself around people, but I also knew I was a part of the athletic community, and that was everything to me.

CHAPTER 8

PASSING MY TEST

MUHAMMAD ALI ONCE SAID, "Champions aren't made in gyms. Champions are made from something they have deep inside them—a desire, a dream, a vision. They have to have the skill and the will. But the will must be stronger than the skill." I love this quote because it has so much meaning I draw inspiration from. Champions are not just made by the amount of time a basketball star spends shooting free throws after practice or the number of times a football player bench-presses 225 at the NFL Combine. They're made from within with desire and commitment to do whatever it takes to succeed. Team champions come from everyone knowing who is on the team, knowing their weaknesses, and striving to perform better—and lifting each other up to perform better. And champions can be everyday people, like me, who hold a vision of excellence for themselves and those around them, even if it doesn't always show on the outside. That is the lasting lesson my final two years as a student athletic trainer taught me.

I came back from Woodward that first summer having learned invaluable lessons that couldn't be found in a textbook. The following spring, I learned more about myself and the kind of person I wanted to become when I was working with the baseball team, which was predicted to be near the top of the MAC. I was paired with another underclassman in his first semester of the program.

Our preceptor, Richard, was a certified graduate student athletic trainer who was in charge of the baseball team. He did not allow us to do much besides grunt work. I never felt part of that team because I felt like what I did for them didn't matter, and I felt judged by Richard. This was most apparent at one of the later practices. He and I were sitting next to the water cooler talking, and he asked me and the other student, "If a girl ever just approached you and wanted to have intercourse with you, would you do it?" I immediately shouted, "No way!" He laughed at me and went around telling all the athletes. Never have I been so embarrassed in my life. But even so, I knew my answer was the right one for me, and I wasn't going to be pressured into giving him an answer he wanted.

Then during the middle of the first game of a double-header, we had a long lightning delay. I was able to hang out in the dugout talking to all the players while we waited to resume the game. After the game ended, I asked Richard if they were going to have a second game since it was so late. We had talked about that possibility earlier. He told me to go ahead and do the end-of-game stuff, such as dump out the water from the visitors' side and clean up both dugouts of cups and other trash. So I went over to the visitors' dugout and dumped the water and started to clean it up when I looked out on the field, and it appeared they were getting ready to start a second game. I knew what I needed to do was take the cart over and fill the cooler up again and bring it back, so I went over to Richard and told him what I was doing before they started the game. He yelled at me—not off to the side but right at me in front of all the student athletes—downgrading me on how stupid and incompetent I was. I wanted to go home and curl up in a ball, but I just bit my tongue and hurried to fix the situation.

I heard later from other students that I was not the only one being treated like this. At the end of the semester, we had to write up a review of our preceptor for that semester. I filled out the front and back of the form with all my complaints against Richard. But as I went to turn it in, I reconsidered. This was his second year and he would not be returning, and it just wasn't in my genes to put someone else down like that. Before I went into my review, I threw the form in the trash. I knew I was better than that. I had gotten out my frustration on paper and that was enough for me.

The next fall, I did a practicum with a physical therapy clinic where I learned about writing up plans and executing those plans with patients. I was placed the following spring semester with the men's and women's track and field teams. That year, our women's team was coming off a close loss the previous season in the conference championships, and they were ready for revenge. The coaches were extremely intense, and it didn't help that the head coach and the assistant had just broken off a long-term relationship with each other. That was a fun dynamic we all got to see play out over the course of that season, but it did teach me more about people.

The indoor track season was something new for me, as we had no chance at my high school to compete running indoors. I also got to travel to some new, cool places with the track teams. My favorite was Harry Gladstein Fieldhouse, the indoor track and field complex in Indianapolis near the Indiana University Natatorium. The indoor track there was a sight to see. Not only was the facility one of the most technologically advanced we had been to, but the track was pristine. One of most impressive parts of that track was that, during some of the sprinting events, the sides flanking the straightaway would be raised using hydraulics to bank the corners as the sprinters ran around them. This helped the runners keep their speed up as they utilized the centripetal force the banks created to sling them around the corners of the track.

My supervising athletic trainer told me I should try to check out the natatorium while we were there, so when there was a lull in the running events, I went over. The natatorium is actually a complex that sits on the Indiana University-Purdue University Indianapolis (IUPUI) campus. Many Olympic qualifying meets are held there, and it's also where some of the Olympic-quality swimmers and divers train. I had been to some amazing pools when I worked with the swimming and diving team, but nothing compared to this pool. The sheer size of the pool—fifty meters compared with Ball State's twenty-five meters—and the clarity of the water stunned me. At the opposite end of the pool, from the springboard height all the way up toward the ceiling to the ten-meter platform; it looked scary enough let alone thinking about jumping off of them into the water.

At the end of the indoor track season, we went to Kent State for the MAC Championship. The women's team dominated the meet, especially in the throwing events, with one woman winning both the weighted throw and the shot put. Our women's sprinting group was so strong that we had won the indoor meet with at least five events to go. No one could have stopped us from winning that day. Off that high, we started the outdoor season. Our champion thrower started to not show up to practices, and it turned out, she had discovered a few days before the indoor meet that she was pregnant. Our second thrower, who probably weighed less than half of our champion, had never even participated in college in some of the events like hammer or javelin. The coaches began getting her up to speed on them, but tensions were high, and we knew we would be giving up her points during the season.

Though we were strong in a lot of the other events, it was going to be tough to win the outdoor meet. However, it was put up or shut up as we entered the Outdoor MAC Championships at Akron near Cleveland. I was not able to see some of our thrower's events because I was dealing with a freshman who had decided that instead of walking two hundred yards around to the entrance of the stadium, he would climb a ten-foot fence and jump off. When he landed, he broke his hand—twenty minutes before he was about to triple-jump, an event he was favored to win. Our female thrower actually earned us some points in her events, but the women's team had only a half-point lead going into the final event, the 1,600-meter relay. Not only is this race always the most exciting event, but this time, there also was so much on the line. We had to take at least third in the event and place at least one spot ahead of Kent State who was behind us. Here's how the relay teams crossed the finish line: Ball State took third and Kent State took fifth. We had won both the indoor and outdoor championships!

After the adversity that team struggled with—losing their star thrower and triple-jump favorite—and with their backs against the wall, they pulled it out. Their grit and determination are what true champions are made of. This was also the first championship team I had the opportunity to be a working part of. A month after that event, the athletic department presented even the student athletic trainers with championship rings. Even though it was not a medal, I did not actually participate in the events, it was my first championship ring, and I treasured it and felt I was a part of the team. I knew I was the one there every day before practice and after practice making sure every one of those athletes delivered their winning performances.

After completing my final sports assignments and clinical rotations, I was near to crossing that finish line my doctor had told me I shouldn't even try to approach. It was time to sit for my national board exam. I had decided two years earlier that I was going to pick up a second major in exercise science when I needed an additional twenty credits to be able to graduate. Since I would only have to take an additional twenty-four credits to earn this second degree, I set out to accomplish this.

The summer before I would graduate in December of 1998, I headed back to Woodward for my second summer there, planning to finish my internship for my exercise science major the coming fall semester. I knew I had to be within a month of graduation when I took the board exam, so I was hitting the books hard studying to take the board exam that November while completing my internship.

Signing up for the exam online the first day I could apply was stressful. Looking at all the sites where I could take it was overwhelming. Most of the ones that were fifteen minutes, two-and-a-half hours, or even six hours away were closed already. The nearest place I could sign up was at Widener University near Philadelphia, thirteen-and-a-half hours away from my home. In the early part of November, my parents drove my brother and me out to the City of Brotherly Love so we could both take the exam.

The exam was split into three sections with sections one and two administered at the same time. While you were taking the written part of the exam, at any point, they could call out your name. When they did, you had to stop where you were, and they escorted you to another room to take section two, the oral practical exam. Anticipating stopping in the middle of an exam to go take another one was beyond stressful. Section three, a written text of responses in different scenarios, was later in the day.

The oral practical exam would test my hands-on skills—some of these were ones I had learned in school and some I had learned at Camp Woodward. I also got pointers from my professors; for example, one of my professors told me not to forget that when I went to do the skills exam, I needed to make sure I either pointed out or tested both sides of the body during the exam. You do this as a trainer to compare the uninjured side of the body with the injured side to help determine the extent of an injury.

We arrived at the test center the morning of the exam around 7:30, well before the exam started at 8. The auditorium was a big lecture hall, but it was packed. We were instructed to have at least one seat open between each other. I ended up sitting toward the top of the auditorium near the aisle. Candidates in the front row were there just to take the oral practical portion for the second time, as the exam was structured such that if you passed one or two out of the three sections, you only had to retake the section(s) you did not pass. As we started the written portion, that row got pulled out first. I knew It would be a while before I got called out.

The written part was about two hundred fifty questions. I remembered a lot of the answers from studying, which I was pretty surprised about, but I quickly noticed there was a section I hadn't given a lot of attention—legal torts. I did my best to answer those questions and reasoned that if I screwed that section up, I needed to make sure to studied those more for the next time. Throughout the written exam, it was constantly in the back of my mind that I was going to be called next. Finally, at about question 180, my name was called.

Switching gears for the oral practical exam was not as bad as I feared. The hardest part was stopping my mind from second-guessing the answers I'd just put down in the written exams. In hindsight, I had needed to focus just on passing this thirty-minute section. The first few parts went by smoothly until I got to the testing and manual muscle section. There were eight parts of that section, and for one part, I remembered how to do the physical test but forgot what it tested for. (Of course, fifteen minutes after I was done, I remembered.) The last test was a test of the biceps tendon in which you turn the palms upward and have the patient raise their arms to chest level. To test both tendons, I ended up doing it at the same time. It was at that moment I realized that for the previous tests, I had forgotten to test on both sides, missing out on points. Again, I took mental notes that if I failed this part by a few points, I would need to make sure I tested both sides next time. Though I knew I missed some points, I felt like I got all the tasks done correctly.

I took the maximum time when I returned to finish the written sections, which probably wasn't the best idea, because I went back through the other answers to double-check myself. People say not to do that, but I did anyway. After a one-hour break, those needing to take section three, the written simulation section, were up next. In this interactive exam, situations are presented and you have to say how you would respond in the field. You are given a highlighter, and after each question or scenario, you highlight your choice of responses from the answers given. Then they give you an update on how the patient or scenario has changed. I breezed through this section for the most part, and three hours later, I was finally done.

I headed to the car where my parents had been hanging out all day. They asked me how it went, and I mentioned the things for sure that I would need to correct if I had to take the test again. My parents had been talking to a few people as they came out about how they felt they had done. My mom said, "Some of the people were taking sections again for the second, third, or fourth times. If you don't pass this time, that's okay." In the back of my mind I knew I wanted to be one and done, but it did make me feel less stressed knowing my parents would not be upset with a failure.

The next week, Kevin and I were finishing up our internships together and waiting for our results. People who had taken it before us said if we got a big package, it meant they were giving us all the information about signing up to retake the sections. If we received just an envelope, it meant we passed.

It was a Friday in December, just two weeks from graduation, when my brother called me from home. His first words were, "We got our letters from the board, and I passed. Do you want me to open yours?" I thought about it for a few minutes. He had already told me that he passed, so did I want him to open mine to tell me that I did not? No. But did I want to wait another four hours not knowing? No way. So I ended up telling him to go ahead.

The next words out of his mouth were, "You passed." I passed the oral practical exam by just a few points, but I knew that was coming, and in the other two sections, I had plenty of room for error. I had done it. I had crossed the finish line. Now I could search for the best place to begin my dream career.

CHAPTER 9

LESSONS FROM
A DETOUR

ANYONE WHO HAS GRADUATED COLLEGE probably remembers the time toward the end when you were trying to decide what you wanted to do and where and for whom. For some, their situations just fall into place. Others might find themselves unready or unwilling to venture too far afield and decide to stay close to home. Maybe an internship you had landed ended up giving you a job that was exactly where you wanted to be. Or maybe the next step was to continue onto grad school to get your master's or doctorate. Maybe you decided traveling the world to find out where you wanted to live was next. Everyone's next step in their journey is different.

Kevin and I graduated in December 1998. Kevin went straight into the workforce, taking a job as an athletic trainer in Crawfordsville, an hour away from Muncie. But I decided to go back to school for my master's degree for more education and training. Few jobs had openings, and I wanted to move away from home eventually.

But for the spring semester in 1999, I attended graduate school at Ball State. I didn't know exactly what classes I wanted to take or even what direction I wanted to go, so I decided to take some general classes and find out. One of my classes changed my mindset on people with disabilities. It was a class on adaptive activities for everyone. The first assignment was to approach someone with a disability and ask them about their story and disability. One of the things I took out of that first lesson was if you approach someone in a wheelchair and start a conversation with them, move down to their eye level, as standing above them creates a stance of superiority.

I began looking for situations where I could talk to others with disabilities and learning how much I was not alone out there. Our class also went to different game nights at the university. At these events, individuals, those with and without disabilities, played games on an even playing field. I soon found out that not only were the guys in wheelchairs every bit as competitive as I was, but some were way faster and more maneuverable than I was. My eyes were opened to the fact that everything can be adapted to include everyone. I also loved the fact that so many of these individuals were there to compete on an even playing field with normal individuals. This was a night I looked forward to the most because it was the first time I was not out-manpowered by able-bodied people who were a lot faster on their feet or stronger than I was.

When I attended Camp Woodward for my third summer after graduation, I was still unsure what I wanted to do, so I casually looked online at teaching assistant jobs. Word got around the camp that I was looking, and one night Mark Stevenson, head women's gymnastics coach at North Carolina State University, approached me and asked if I would be interested in a graduate assistant athletic training job at his university. Mark was such a great individual when we worked together at camp that I said, "Why not?" I applied, got the job, and left Woodward that summer and headed to Raleigh, North Carolina.

I thought about teaching, sports information, or sports recreation but had no guidance on classes or programs at the university. I could not get anyone to help direct me unless I was accepted into a program, and the ones I wanted to get into all told me I needed a higher GRE score. I was not a great standardized test taker. I got the bare minimum on the SAT and ACT after two tries before getting into undergrad. But my grades in high school were a 3.55 and a 3.6 in college, so I knew I could do the work. That first semester, I ended up taking a bunch of different courses just to get an idea what I might be interested in.

On a positive note, I enjoyed working with the gymnastics team. Mark made me feel at home with him, and being the athletic trainer for the team was rewarding. Part of the job was working for the sports medicine team, and that was a completely different story. Being a recent grad, I had not been exposed to the logistics regarding getting athletes looked at or procuring things I felt they needed. I found out quickly that my team was not the priority. For things like ordering someone orthotics for their running shoes or even scheduling someone to be seen by a physician, the basketball and football teams took first priority and my girls did not. Numerous times I was questioned why I was taking up space in the training room when I knew I was doing certain things with athletes that would help them.

Second semester, I decided to go the teaching route because I felt that could always be a backup with my condition. If I ever wanted to teach athletic training, I could, even with my disability. Before I signed up for my classes, I noticed one of them was at the same time as the beginning of gymnastics practice. I approached our head athletic trainer and asked if it would be okay if I took that class. He fixed his eyes on me and said, "If that class is going to interfere with your being with gymnastics, you should probably rethink what your major is going to be." I had been searching for someone to help me figure out what I wanted to do. With that one sentence, I realized this was not the place I wanted to be, and I would need to take matters in my own hands.

I knew that semester was going to be a busy one with all the travel we had coming up during the season with gymnastics, so I decided to take only one class in teaching, which was the minimum to keep my scholarship with the university. I withdrew from the other classes because I knew I was not planning on returning after that year. Fulfilling my obligation to Mark and his team was the only thing that was keeping me there.

I had a blast that year as we traveled up and down the East Coast and even to Bermuda. Midway through the semester in my teaching class, the teacher approached me after class and asked me why I did not complete more classes and finish my application to the program. I was honest with him that I had been told my GRE scores were not high enough to apply and no one would talk to me about any program until that changed. He said, "I wish you would have sought me out. Your grades in my class and your grades from college would have been sufficient to be accepted into the graduate college of teaching." As I explained everything else, he said he understood why I had made my decision.

I kept my decision of what I was doing at the end of the semester from Mark because I did not want him to judge me for it, and I wasn't about to cross the line and tell him about my bad experience with the education department and how I felt about the sports medicine department. Would it have made me feel better about my decision? Yes, but would it have made any difference in my decision? No, it would not have. All I wanted to do was enjoy the meets and the places we went to and finish the year and start over. The women's team was one of the strongest Mark had. For them to be ranked fifteenth to twentieth in the country that year was a crazy ride. When we competed at the Ohio State University, my parents were able to attend.

In Florida, we stayed at the Marriott at Sawgrass; I recognized the name but didn't know why. It was not until I got to my room that first afternoon and looked out the window that I saw we were right on a golf course. As I panned down, I saw "TPC Sawgrass" spelled out in the formation of the bushes. It was The Players Championship course I used to watch every year. I remembered one of the most famous and feared holes on the PGA tour—the seventeenth hole, a 132-yard par-3 island green hole. I don't remember what our teams scored or even if we won our match at the University of Florida or not. All I remember was going out the next day to try to make it to the seventeenth hole. Early in the morning I woke up and walked into the golf course clubhouse and asked the pro there if there was any way I could go out and just take some pictures of the seventeenth hole. He said if I waited around a little bit, he might be able to take me out, but I couldn't go right then because they were getting ready for the US Open and were limiting the number of people on the course.

As I waited around, I looked at a board with the names and pictures of all the TPC winners, including Greg Norman, Fred Couples and, of course, Tiger Woods. I had been waiting about an hour when a random member heard I was wanting to go out. He drove me out in a golf cart, and I saw the seventeenth green plus many of the other holes I'd seen on TV. The fascination for me was every year I watched players on this course, and I always pictured myself playing from the spots the professionals did. Even though I could never drive the ball as far as they did or putt as well as they did, I loved imagining what that would feel like to be there playing. Seeing it in person and walking on the same grass as those legends was amazing to experience.

We ended the regular season and headed to the University of Pittsburgh for the Eagle Conference Championship as the favorites, ranked fifteenth in the country. All we needed to do was not have to count any falls and we would win the championship. We had finished our last event, which was floor exercise. The scoring was very close between Maryland in second and us. We had a bye, and by the last round, we had not counted a fall the entire meet. Maryland didn't have one either up to that point. They finished their event on the beam, and their first girl up, which typically is a team's weaker person, fell on her routine. We knew they could throw out one score in every event and this would probably be it. Then the fourth girl slipped off the beam when she went to land her tumbling sequence. As she moved to get back up on the beam to finish her routine, she called her coach, Bob Nelligan, over and they noticed a split in the beam.

After that was fixed, she was able to redo her event and, of course, she hit it. But then the last girl in the event ended up falling also. When the final scores came up, we had won the 2000 Eagle Conference Championship, the second championship team I was a part of.

After they announced we won, I jumped for joy inside. Even though I was not up there on the beam or twisting and making landings coming off the bars, I was proud knowing I had been there to help those girls back from many injuries during the year. After they got their award, I stood behind everyone, offering to take team photos with all their phones. Even though I wanted so badly to get one of me with them, I stood back and didn't force myself into the situation. I think it was partly out of my insecurity over the difficulties I had that year. As I was snapping through all the phones, one of the athletes on the team yelled out, "Could someone please take some of those cameras so Kurt can come and get in the picture with us? He was a part of this too." All the girls chimed in to encourage me to come and be in the picture with them. That feeling of being accepted and being part of the team was the best.

Though I really enjoyed being with the team, I did not have any guidance through the university and did not get any support from the athletic trainers at the university. There were some great things that came out of that year, but at the end of the semester, I was excited to get out of there. That same year, three other GAs and two staff members also left early because of the situation, which made me feel better that I was not the only one. I left Raleigh early in the morning and headed back to Camp Woodward to see where life would take me next.

Once I got there, I again searched online for jobs and worked on my résumé. Throughout that summer of 2000, a woman from the New England area was randomly coming in and hanging out in our training room. She was a former Division III gymnast outside of Philadelphia. She was there that summer biding time before she started her new job as head coach at the University of Wisconsin at Oshkosh. As the weeks went on, we hung out more and more, as at camp, you spend most of your day either in the dining hall, at the pool, or in the gym. We got to know each other really well at camp and fell in love. So I began looking for jobs in Wisconsin.

Midway through summer, I got two interviews and took a week off to go home then head up to Wisconsin. These were my first real job interviews. The first one was near Oshkosh working for Affinity Health Group Orthopedics, and there were three other people applying for the same job. I asked how long it would be until we knew, and they said it would be a few weeks before any decision would be made. That night, my parents and I drove to Kenosha for my other interview, for a job working with industrial workman's comp injuries part of the day and at a local high school in the afternoons. After that interview, I was shocked they offered me the job on the spot. I didn't know what to do, so I asked if I could think it over for the night. When I got to my car, I called my parents to discuss both jobs. The first thing my mom said was, "Are you sure this is what you want do and where you want to move to?"

I always knew I wanted to live away from my hometown, and I was not a homebody like my brother was. One of the summers I was in Pennsylvania, Kevin tried working as a temporary employee at a hockey camp at Miami of Ohio. The longest camp week they had was five days, and being away from home that long was too much for him. When he got his AT job in Crawfordsville, we moved him into an apartment right after Christmas, but three weeks later, he got homesick and moved back to Muncie, where he still lives today. So when my mom asked me her question, I knew she wanted to make sure she would not be moving me back in a month's time from five hours away. On the way back home, I thought of that situation. But the more I thought about it, I knew I didn't want to live in Muncie. I loved the town and my family and friends, but I also wanted to get to know more people outside my hometown. I called the Kenosha place up the next day and told them I would take the job, once again proving my doctor wrong and crossing another finish line.

CHAPTER 10

MY FIRST JOB AS AN ATHLETIC TRAINER

THAT FIRST DAY ON THE JOB, all my doubts about my condition and connecting with people came out in full force: Will I be accepted for my skills and attitude? Or judged for my disability? Will anyone notice my limitations? At this point there wasn't much I couldn't do physically, but some things I had just started were harder for me to do—jogging out onto the field during games.

The job at Kenosha's Bradford High School was an eye opener. I knew nothing about the town or even about the area, let alone the school. I was told to show up around seven for football practice. I arrived a little early so I could try to see where things were. But as the athletes started to arrive, I could tell I was in a different community compared to the little country school I'd attended in Indiana. This school reminded me more of the inner-city community where my dad went to school. The police presence was my first clue; we never had a cop at our school. Then the amount of different races and ethnicities I saw in just the first few hours struck me. I knew from working with all my athletes that every one of these kids had a story and I just needed to be part of it. I soon found out that many of the kids were sent to Bradford because the other schools in the district could not control them.

There also were sports at Bradford I had not worked with yet. The one I wanted to learn the most about was soccer. Early on I was sitting on the sidelines at a game, and while the kids were playing, one of the JV soccer coaches started teaching me the ins and outs of the game. At first, I thought I could not wait for the games to be over with. But even though our team was not very good, I started enjoying the games as the year went on.

As the school year progressed, I learned the dynamics of the athletes' parents. At one event, I ran out to help an injured player. After I got him off to the sidelines, I asked him if his parents were in the stands. He said they were not. I was sad to find out that was pretty much the norm. Growing up in the country in Indiana, on Friday nights, every parent and even grandparents came to the kids' football games. Even my parents used to go to the football games, and all I did was play in the band, and when I was a manager for the cross-country and basketball teams, my parents always made an effort to come watch the event even though I wasn't participating. I knew through working at Ball State and North Carolina State, parents used to travel from all over to their kids' events. Not seeing the parents at events made me feel for these kids, even though I understood many of them were working extra hours to be able to provide for their families. It made me try harder to be supportive of the athletes. It also made me grateful to my parents for being at my events. I knew I had needed them there. This was the first time I realized not all kids get to have that essential element of support.

Living on my own for the first time, I learned a lot about myself, especially with cooking. When you're cooking Hamburger Helper (my favorite bachelor meal), for instance, you should not eat the entire box in one sitting. I learned that the hard way, ballooning from 190 to 225 pounds in a few months. Even though I lived in an apartment, which was relatively easy to maintain, I had to learn to pay bills and do a lot of things on my own. The one thing I loved doing around Kenosha, which is just north of Chicago and south of Milwaukee and sits right along the shoreline of Lake Michigan, was riding my bike. I would often ride along the shoreline thinking of different things that were going on in my life and pondering my job, relationships, and, always, how I was handling my condition.

For six years after my diagnosis, I kept a lot about it to myself. Even so, many people I knew casually or the athletes I worked with would sometimes ask me, "What is wrong with your legs or your knees?" I would tell them that I had bad knees since I was young. A lot of my reticence was due to my desire to be treated like everyone else. One afternoon I had just finished riding the velodrome in town and had decided to make my way down to the lake. I was thinking back on all I had accomplished since I was first diagnosed: working at the Finish Line for five years and being one of their top sellers, year in and year out; being able to work with some of the top extreme sports athletes at Camp Woodward and even getting a job offer to go on tour with the Vans Warped Tour; winning two championship rings with two different collegiate teams; passing my boards on the first try and landing my first job. I had come so far. Then I got to thinking of all the stories of hardship at Kenosha Bradford and of my dad's tough life as a young adult in Muncie and my parents' struggles through the years. Everyone has something in life to deal with, and what is important is how we respond to adversity and strive to improve ourselves and help those around us.

I thought it might be time to allow people into my life and let them know the real me. Maybe I could use my example to help others come to see that no matter who we are, we are normal in God's eyes and he sees us as his beloved children. I decided to be more open about my condition if people asked, but I still acknowledged it only if people asked. I realized telling people about what I was going through might allow me to connect with them on a different level and might even be of some service to them.

When I was working Bradford football games, I followed the action running up and down the sidelines; my theory was if someone went down, I would not be very far away and would not have to run very far to reach them. In the fall of my second year, I noticed that running had become difficult. I tried hiding it as much as I could, but one Friday night, one of my football players got injured. I ran out, trying my best to get to him as fast as I could. I was pumping my arms, but by my feet were not going as fast as my hands, and I was unable to pick my legs up quickly, so it felt more like a fast-walking pace. I noticed one of the athletes was mimicking my running, which embarrassed me. It reminded me of my days in school when kids would come up behind me and hit the back of my knees because they knew I could not keep myself from falling. Even though I did not know anything about my condition back then, their laughter always made me feel defeated. When I saw the player mocking me, it instantly took me back there. Once I reached the hurt player, I focused on what I needed to do to help him, but that defeated feeling lingered.

I realized how much my body was reacting to my condition in my second basketball season at Bradford. The gym was so big they could have practices for wrestling, gymnastics, and boys' or girls' freshman through varsity basketball teams all at one time. On nights of events, they pulled the bleachers into the middle to surround the main court. And the entire facility was covered with a rubber type of surface, the same as its indoor track.

In college when I worked with all the sports teams, I dressed to match the coaching staff. One night, at a Bradford boys' basketball game, an athlete was injured on the court and I went out to evaluate him. After I was done, he went back to the bench and I started to get up but couldn't. For those of you reading this who have SMA, you know what I'm talking about. When I get up, I push my feet out behind me and use my hands to push up, as my legs try to get locked into extension. Then I walk my hands down my legs until they're straight up and down. I can then bend my waist backward to stand up. I had never had an issue, but that night my shoes were sliding on the rubber floor, so I was unable to get my knees straightened to stand up. I was frozen out on the court by myself. Luckily, I was near the side where the bleachers were, so I crawled over and was able to hoist myself up to the first row. Some of the students started laughing, which made me feel very low.

After two years at Kenosha, I got married then landed a job in Oshkosh, Wisconsin, with Affinity Health Group, who had been my first interview two years before. They actually remembered me and hired me on the spot. My job there was as a practice assistant with an orthopedic surgeon. Though I felt out of my element at first, I caught on early and thoroughly enjoyed working for my physician, and over the course of a year, we became pretty close friends. I also was working for a small school outside Appleton called Little Chute High School. That first football season I followed the team closely and went to many of their away games, which was not in my job description. The conference championship came down to the final game, and we ended up beating a team that had only one loss to our two losses and finishing the season with a four-way tie for first place.

My wife and I moved to Perrysburg, Ohio (a suburb of Toledo), to be near her job. I took a job mainly working at a local high school and occasionally at the rehab facility at St. Luke's Hospital assisting the physical therapist. It was considered part time, but I was told they'd see about increasing my hours to full time. Within a month, I inquired about going full time and was told it would never happen, so I stayed in contact with another place that was on a hiring freeze at the time; I told them if something opened up to please contact me. All this uncertainty left me feeling inadequate about providing for my family, and I second-guessed leaving Wisconsin. I prayed that God would give me the opportunity to get a full-time job. He answered that prayer about two months later, and I left the hospital job to work full time with ProMedica Bay Park Hospital and Northwood High School.

CHAPTER 11

ADOPTING MY DAUGHTER

FOR THE MOST PART, I was comfortable with my career, engaged with employers, students, and clients alike, and I loved my work and felt good doing it. It was time to invest in my family relationships. After working in Ohio for about a year, my wife and I began discussing having kids. Knowing what I had gone through with my condition, I did not want to take a chance on it getting passed to my children. We looked into adoption, and after much research and discussion, we settled on adopting a child in Russia. We went through the America World Adoption Association (AWAA), which had agencies all over the United States. The one we used in Findlay, Ohio, was run by a husband-and-wife team who made us feel at ease with the process.

Over the next several months, we had to collect numerous forms and data for our dossier. We needed three different home inspections; three interviews with a social worker; a fire inspection; finger printing by state, FBI, and international offices; a psychological test; plus a list of all our financial information. The process took about five months to pull everything together and was costly too. We were fortunate my parents generously helped us financially.

My biggest fear was worrying my SMA condition would disqualify me in the eyes of the courts and/or agency and they wouldn't approve me to be a father. Though there was nothing I couldn't do to take care of a child, I feared they might consider the long-term question marks of my condition to be risky enough to not approve me. Maybe, too, they would think that down the road I would not be able to financially take care of a child if I was unable to work.

I had disclosed my condition to Mike Stone, our agent with AWAA. I told him there was no cure and no certainty of what my condition would look like in the future, but at the time I was more than able to take care of a kid. He told me not to mention the SMA in my home study and I should be fine, but the questions kept swirling in my mind.

Then on Christmas Eve 2005, we placed all the information in an envelope and sent it out. Within two months we got an email with a picture attached of a beautiful eighteen-month-old girl standing in front of a wall, a small tear in her eyes. Looking through her history, I noticed that her birthday was two days after mine. I had always shared a birthday with my twin, but after moving away from home, I had realized it was kind of nice not having to share it. But as soon as I saw her birthday was so close to mine, I felt glad I was going to be sharing a birthday with this little girl. Then I looked at her name, Vera, which means "faith" in Russian. Since my diagnosis, faith had pulled me through some of the hardest times, and God had continually shown me that all I needed to do was have faith. God was showing me faith in the form of a little girl on the other side of the world, and all I needed now was to go get her.

Two weeks after receiving all of Vera's information, my wife and I were on a flight to Krasnoyarsk, Russia, in central Siberia. Hopping on a plane to go to a foreign country is tough enough, let alone having to stop in the middle of Germany (an eight-hour flight) to switch planes to head to Moscow (four-hour flight) then get on another plane to fly into Krasnoyarsk. The language barrier was difficult too, but once we got to Moscow, we had an interpreter to guide us and take us where we needed to go. Krasnoyarsk was smaller and less developed than Moscow. At the airport, I felt I had seen the place before. Soon I realized it was the same airport as in the movie *Rocky IV* (released in 1985) when Rocky Balboa flies to Russia to fight Apollo Creed, the Soviet boxer.

The couple who would be the agency's representatives while we were there met us at the airport, and after dropping off our stuff at the hotel, we were whisked away for our visit with our potential daughter. The gamut of emotions rolled through me on the drive. I wanted to take in the scenery, but all I could think about was how Vera might react to us. Will she like us? Will she be afraid of us as strangers? I also worried about making a good impression on the caregivers and the orphanage director who would eventually advocate for us in court.

The worst fear was wondering if the powers that be would see that I had a disability and reject us because of it. Would they see that I was unable to stand from a chair without utilizing my hands to push me up? If we were in the orphanage and we got on the ground, would the director or caregivers take notice that I got up off the floor awkwardly? Would they notice that I would not be able to stand up from a couch while holding a child? Or would they notice that I had to hold onto two rails as I ascended and descended stairs, pulling or pushing on the rail in order to get my legs onto each step? All the things I'd been painfully aware of as an issue for many years now loomed very large.

The plain brick building we pulled up to did not look like my idea of an orphanage. The only evidence that kids lived here were the tire swings in a courtyard outside and a woman pushing a stroller on the grounds with five toddlers holding hands following behind. Inside, they instructed us to put on shoe covers, which made my feet slippery as I walked up the steps, adding to my nervousness.

We entered a huge playroom sparsely outfitted with a piano, large foam shapes for climbing, and dozens of toys grouped to one side. We sat on a couch in a corner waiting for them to bring Vera to us. The door finally opened, and one of the caregivers brought her into the room and started to hand her to my wife, but the child's chin puckered up and tears fell. She pushed my wife away from her, so the caregiver sat next to her and fed her dinner. Between each bite, we could hear her whimpering. When the child was done eating, the caregiver left and immediately Vera reached out after her. As she began to calm down, we played with her on the floor, letting her pick up things and stack them over and over. What seemed like half an hour ended up being two, but I had known as soon as she was brought into the room that this would be my daughter.

With our representatives' help, we navigated the Russian bureaucracy and got the papers signed, including adding the name we had contemplated since receiving her photo and information, Mikayla Vera-Nicole Beach. We knew we wanted to keep her original name, and Mikayla had stuck with us after watching the Olympics before we left for Russia and marveling at the strength and speed of downhill skier Michaela Dorfmeister. Her name carried our wish for our daughter to become just as strong.

We went home that night exhausted from the travels and emotions of the day and finally meeting the child who was going to be our first child. After a strange breakfast of sausages that resembled hot dogs, packaged casseroles that appeared to be eggs, and pastries—we bypassed the odd combinations on the buffet of corn, peas, and salad—we headed back for the last day we would be able to spend time with Mikayla before returning to the United States. As soon as she came in, she again clung to the caregiver and started crying. My wife was able to take her this time, however, and she calmed down quickly.

At the orphanage, everyone was female, so Mikayla had never seen a man and she was too wary to come to me. We tried tricking her as she was playing, distracting her then switching so she would be sitting on my lap. She began to be okay with me as long as my wife was right there next to her.

We also got to tour the facility to see where Mikayla slept in a room with close to twenty-five other cribs and where she played with the rest of the kids her age. My favorite part was seeing her climb up into the middle of a castle, wait her turn, then slide down the slide head first. Halfway down, she spread her legs out to the sides trying to slow or stop herself as she neared the bottom. We sat and watched the kids playing, and it broke my heart hearing all those kids call us Mom and Dad.

Too soon, it was time to go. I instantly started to cry at the thought we wouldn't see Mikayla for months until we came back to go to court. At the end of our visit, as she was taken away, I lost it. One year after making the decision to pursue adoption, a prayer had become a reality, and she, our child, was here in front of me. Now I had to leave her and pray that our bond would hold until we came back. She had my heart, the heart of a father for his daughter.

What was supposed to be a three-month wait turned into four, then finally at five months we got a court date and headed back to get her. The next hurdle was our court appearance. We were prepped by the lawyer and the AWAA people, who prepared us for some of the questions and told us what we should say in response to them. We rehearsed our answers with them, and I practiced those responses most of the night. I still worried if my condition would be noticed or become a factor.

The only question that threw me a bit was when the judge unexpectedly mentioned our pet boxers and asked what we would do if the dogs got rough with Mikayla. I immediately responded we would protect our daughter by either training them or getting rid of the dogs. The whole time I was nervous wondering if the judge would see anything amiss with how I walked or got out of my chair, but nothing was mentioned. The judge approved our adoption after about fifteen minutes of deliberation. I was finally a father, and my parents had their first grandchild. Mikayla Vera-Nicole Beach was coming to America.

CHAPTER 12

REDISCOVERING AND DEEPENING LOVE AND FAITH

THE WEEK WE CAME BACK FROM RUSSIA, I asked for a transfer to a new school near Toledo. The school was a little farther east of where we lived, but when I entered the town of Swanton and saw all the purple and white, I knew I was home. It reminded me of my dad bleeding purple and white for the Muncie Central Bearcats. My brother was the trainer there now, too, so I had been the odd man out at Christmas with everyone but me getting purple and white jerseys and trinkets. Now I had a purple and white school of my own to call home in Swanton, Ohio.

I had everything I could have wished for with a job and family I loved. But, of course, there were challenges. Because Mikayla didn't have a male figure in her twenty-two months of life, she was struggling to slowly get used to me, and her fears put more pressure on my wife. Whenever she left Mikayla to go to work or run errands or have some time to herself, Mikayla would cry and pull at her to try and make her stay. My wife usually just took her with her on errands because it was so stressful. I took Mikayla out in the stroller in the afternoons during her naptime so my wife could take a shower or just get a break. And when I finished work early, I was able to get Mikayla from daycare. As soon as I would enter the room, despite the joy showing plainly on my face, Mikayla would start crying because it was not her mom picking her up. I did my best just to be patient and never give up on knowing she would come around to me.

Things did get a little easier as time passed, and Mikayla learned to trust me. I was able to take her with me on my own errands. As soon as we exited the car in a parking lot, she waited for me then grabbed my hand and walked next to me the entire time. We were taking it day by day, and I didn't realize it was taking a toll on my wife.

Looking back, I can see I got complacent with my marriage as my focus shifted to my daughter and helping her get used to me. I stopped noticing that things were not right with my wife. One evening we were all sitting down for dinner, she asked me if we could go to counseling. In denial, I thought to myself that I did not need counseling; there was nothing wrong. A week after she saw the counselor by herself, she told me she was moving out for a while just to get a breather. I now had to realize and acknowledge something was wrong.

That following week, we both met with the counselor. When we walked into the office, I was aware for the first time since we had gotten married of how distant she was. We sat down, and the counselor asked us what was going on. My wife pulled out a piece of paper and began reading a letter she had written. As she began reading the letter, my heart sank. She ended the letter telling me that she had moved on and wanted a divorce. The counselor's look was just as puzzled as mine. I thought we were there to work things out, but it was just for her to tell me she was done.

I never wanted to be on the wrong side of divorce statistics in America, but here I was. After a few attempts on my part to reconcile and many nights of prayer asking God to bring her back to me, I finally had to realize the marriage was over. I felt my life was in shambles; I was trying to swim but couldn't keep my head above water. I felt okay for stretches at a time, but every so often, I found myself gasping for breath. Even though I kept up my workouts at the gym, my body started to waste away. I also was eating as normally as I could, but every few months, when I felt more stressed, I lost another five or six pounds. At night it was harder and harder to stay asleep, and I would wake up in the middle of the night crying.

Questions haunted me: What was I going to do with my life? Where was I going to go from here? Would I ever find someone again who would accept me for me—and would they want to be with someone with a disability? Sometimes, I must confess, I wondered if it was even worth continuing with my life. Fortunately, every time I thought that, I knew there was one thing I was sure of—I had a little girl who needed a father, no matter how unstable he might be feeling. Mikayla needed a dad, and I knew I wanted to be there for her as a strong, loving, present father.

I realized I needed help and began seeing my primary care physician, who told me after our first visit, that she had gone through the same thing. She gave me some medications to help me sleep and help me with the depression I was experiencing. I also began seeing a counselor who walked me through the steps to cope with the situation and get my life back on track.

Most important, I started to pay attention to my relationship with God again. After we came back from Russia, we had stopped going to church as often. I now began attending our First United Methodist Church, taking Mikayla with me on Sunday nights for children's group. I also taught whenever they needed someone, and my favorite times were when I led Mikayla's class. I developed a few relationships there and was beginning to regain a trust with God I thought I had lost.

One day I was going through some of my CDs and found one by a contemporary artist I had seen when I was in the youth group back in Muncie. I listened to the whole CD one week, and it made me think of a church in the area that I knew sang more contemporary songs. I started attending a contemporary nondenominational church as well as the Methodist church with Mikayla every Sunday. In the contemporary church, I felt God's presence most, not only through the songs but also in the messages from the pastor, which seemed to be spoken especially for me.

After only my second service at the contemporary church, a man who had taken care of Mikayla the previous Sunday in children's church invited me to join his life group, and I dove deeper into the word of God in that group. A few weeks later, I talked to Rex Stump with Fellowship of Christian Athletes (FCA), who had been coming to Swanton to speak to football players after their practices about leadership and diversity. I told him one day about this CD I had listened to and how much it meant to me, and he brought me several burned CDs of other contemporary Christian songs.

One night I was on a date with a woman I had met at the Methodist church. We were sitting and talking outside on a bench. She pulled a small Bible out of her purse and began reading from it. I knew I needed my own Bible that was small enough to leave in my car so it would always be near, but I didn't know where to start looking for one, so I just put the thought in the back of my mind.

The next day was a Thursday. Usually Rex came on Mondays, but that week he was there on Thursday. Toward the end of practice, Rex came up and handed me a stack of CDs plus a box. I left them on the seat of the Gator I rode around in at practice so I could hear his message to the athletes. After he was done speaking, I walked back to see what he had brought me. I shuffled through the CDs and got to the box and opened it. It was a hand-sized, FCA, leather-bound Bible meant for athletes. God does indeed work in mysterious ways. In that moment, I realized God was listening to me and supporting me. He was always there listening, but sometimes he had a different plan than I did. After that, things began to change.

I knew I needed to be with someone who was a Christian and held Christianity also themselves but didn't even know where to begin. I was never a bar kind of person, especially since I never drank. I remembered that, before my divorce, at my brother's wedding, he had mentioned he had met his wife on a dating app. I was kind of skeptical about dating online, but I thought it was worth a try.

I went on many dates the first few weeks and began to develop relationships, even though many of them fizzled out over time. Either our views didn't match up, or the women were too young, or we were in different stages of our lives and didn't seem to fit together. After a five-month relationship ended, I went back on the dating site, and a young lady from Canton, Michigan, began talking to me. After a few emails and phone conversations, I eventually asked her if she wanted to meet. Surprising me, she actually said yes.

The next week I drove up and met her in Canton. The weather was sunny and warm, which was unusual for March in our area. Driving into town and trying to find a parking spot on a Thursday night was a nightmare. I couldn't figure out why it was so busy until I noticed the people wearing leprechaun hats and shamrock eyeglasses as well as people sporting Michigan State gear. It hit me—it was St. Patrick's Day, and MSU was playing in the Sweet 16 of the NCAA March Madness basketball tournament.

Eventually I found a spot and made it to the restaurant to meet Leeann for the first time. I felt like I had gotten to know her as much as I could over the phone, but thinking about actually seeing her in person made me nervous. Would she notice how I walk or how I get out of a chair and reject me? I prayed to God that I would not trip and fall while we were together and that all would go well.

She had also had difficulty finding a parking spot. We arrived at the restaurant at the same time but from opposite directions. All I knew about what she looked like for sure was she had blonde hair, blue eyes, and a bright smile. Even from a distance, walking toward each other, I could see that it was her. I totally forgot about myself and my doubts as we ate and easily talked about everything, including my daughter and my job. We also talked about her mom, who was in the hospital with a stroke and whose health had deteriorated to the point that she was unable to talk. Leeann's concern for her mom was evident.

Later we walked all around town as Leeann showed me the ins and outs of where she lived. We ended up sitting and talking on a bench near the center of town, and by then, I knew I was falling for this girl. At the end of the night, I was wondering what I was going to do to say goodbye. Should I hug her, fist-bump with her, or give her a handshake? I didn't want to scare her off. As we parted, I reached over and gave her a hug. On the ninety-minute drive home, all I could do was think about her. Just as I crossed over the border into Ohio, I got a text from Leeann asking if I'd gotten home okay yet, thanking me for an amazing date, and saying it was the best one she had gone on in a while. My heart sang with those unforgettable words.

Our second date wasn't until a few weeks later—to a furniture place to look at couches for the house I had just moved into. As we were walking through the store, Leeann came up beside me, and as our hands brushed, we wrapped our fingers together. As the months passed, Leeann and I were definitely falling in love with each other. Leeann wanted me to meet her mom, Nancy, in the hospital, because she wasn't sure she would ever come home. I was nervous, worrying what I would say to her since she couldn't answer me back or speak at all. But then I remembered a class I had in college on adaptive physical education for everyone, which was about developing programming for people with disabilities. One of our assignments early on in the class was going up to random people who had a disability and striking up a conversation with them about their disability. Being someone with a disability, I totally related to them, and I knew treating them as I would like to be treated was the key.

Leeann called me into Nancy's hospital room, and as I walked along the foot of the bed to stand by her, her mom's eyes widened. Leeann gave her a hug, and I saw Nancy was looking at me with a huge smile on her face. After Leeann introduced us, she waved me over to come sit next to her, lightly pushing her daughter to the side. We still laugh about how adamant she was to have me near her that day. For about an hour, I chatted about my parents, my job, and the adoption of my daughter, and Leeann filled her mom in on her life and people they knew. It was wonderfully normal.

The next few months I spent as much time as I could manage with Leeann and her parents. Leeann's mom did get to go home, but after several weeks at home, she got her angel wings. Getting to know Leeann and her family during this sad time, I was sure this was the girl I was meant to spend the rest of my life with. I proposed to Leeann on July 3, 2011, and we were married on March 18 the next year, one year and a day after our first date.

A month or two after the wedding, we were visiting my parents and brother and sister-in-law in Indiana. While my mom and dad where getting things ready for dinner, Kevin said that they had been trying to have kids with no luck. He had been tested and discovered he was infertile. He was telling us because, if we wanted to have kids, I should get tested to see if I might have the same issue. My wife definitely wanted a child, and I was ready to give her one, so when we got back to Toledo, I got tested. I got the call at work and had my dreams dashed by another doctor when he told me I was infertile. I asked my boss if I could go outside and call my wife. After telling her the news, my next words were, "If you want to leave me now, I would rather not wait and suffer being unable to give you what you want." I'll always remember how Leeann responded. "I am with you for the long haul; you can't get rid of me," she said. "We are in this together and we will make it through this and figure it out."

We spent the next few months trying to figure it out, eventually landing on embryo adaption, where the doctors would take someone else's fertilized eggs and place them in Leeann. The process of multiple shots and medications Leeann had to take over several months was intense and expensive. Finally, we had embryos implanted a few weeks after Valentine's Day in 2014. We waited, wondering if it was going to work, until March 26 when we had a video call with the fertility clinic. We were excited but anxious to know if we would be parents. The words that came out of the doctor's mouth were not what we had hoped for.

"The embryo did not attach, and I'm sorry that you are not pregnant," he said. Leeann squeezed my hand hard, and I could tell she was holding in tears.

The next few weeks, we processed our emotions and talked about our next step. It came down to our agreeing we had spent a lot of money that many people had donated to us to help cover the costs, and we just didn't feel trying again would be worth it. We looked into Mikayla's eyes, who was now seven years old, and decided to see if the process that had brought her to me would work a second time.

We went through all the classes and certifications to become foster or adoptive parents. First, we intended to adopt the foster child of someone Leeann's family knew. But in seven months, a court date to make her eligible for adoption kept getting postponed. One day, a close family friend called Leeann about an email she received from a couple "looking for a loving adoptive-minded family to adopt our soon-to-be-born child." Leeann said we were interested on the spot, and the friend responded to the family, telling them about us and how Mikayla was adopted from Russia.

We spoke with the couple that night on the phone, and we could not have asked anything to go smoother. At the end of the conversation, the birth father and mother said they would like for us to adopt their soon-to-be-born child. The mother would be going the next day for her first ultrasound to find out how far along she was.

She said she was maybe six months along. The next day, she sent us a text to let us know that the baby was healthy—and was due to be born in about two weeks!

We went into hyper mode getting everything ready in the house for this child to come, as well as preparing and completing all the paperwork. One thing that was concerning me that my wife did not know was that, even though we had saved some of the donated money from our embryo adoption, we were still $1,000 short of the fees we needed to finalize the adoption. One Sunday afternoon, Kristin, a close friend of Leeann we had done life group together with, called to say she and her husband had some things for us. Many of our friends had started to give us baby things they had kept from when their kids were born, so we thought this would be clothes they had saved for us. My wife met them later that night in the parking lot of our church and Kristin handed her an envelope. Leeann called me to say she was on her way home and told me Kristin had given her a check for $1,000. I then told my wife that was the exact amount we needed. It was another miracle and more proof God was watching over us.

A few weeks later, doctors induced labor of our soon-to-be-child. We were staying in Ann Arbor with Leeann's aunt and uncle in their new home because Michigan statutes said we stay in the same county as Mott's Children's Hospital (part of the University of Michigan medical center) until the court gave us permission to take the child home. My wife's birthday was a few days after the doctors were inducing labor, so we decided to have dinner at The Cheesecake Factory then drive around Ann Arbor shopping for several things we still needed. We hadn't received a call, so we went back to the house to wait it out.

At 12:30 in the morning, Leeann got a call from the birth father telling us that our baby boy had arrived. We were instantly awake, gathered all our stuff, and headed to the hospital.

We were both a bundle of nerves, thrilled to be seeing our son but still filled with doubts. Will the couple change their minds about allowing us to adopt the child she had just given birth to? Will everything be okay with the baby physically? We knocked on the door, and the birth father opened it, welcoming us into the room. My wife had said she wanted to first console the mother, even before seeing the baby, to make her feel at ease and let her know we were so thankful for the sacrifice she was making. But as Leeann approached the bed, the birth mother handed her our little, perfect baby boy. My wife's eyes glistened with joy. I hadn't seen her face shine like that for almost a year, through all our struggles.

As we sat and talked with the family that early morning, Leeann leaned over to me and whispered in my ear, "Do you realize what day it is?" It was March 26; a year before to the day, we got the call from the fertility clinic that our embryo adoption had failed, and we were crushed with uncertainty that a new child would be in our lives. Now we could remember it as the day that Colton Mathew-Hudson Beach would be our son for eternity.

Having a newborn was new for us both since Mikayla was twenty-two months old when she came home. Four days after leaving the hospital, at a checkup, Leeann pulled off Colton's diaper, and he decided to have a bowel movement directly into my wife's hand. But not an ounce of poop even hit the bed. Although my wife has never been good at sports or even catching a ball, that day would have made any coach proud.

In the early weeks, Colton became a part of our family. The deadline for the parents to be able to change their mind about our adopting him passed. We were so anxious to get the paperwork from the courts that officially changed his last name to ours and to determine his Gotcha Day. This is a tradition among adoptive families, designating the day the courts officially declare a child the ward of the adoptive families as their Gotcha Day. I had celebrated Mikayla's since she was brought to the States.

Finally, one day in mid-August we received mail from the courthouse in Michigan. Not only did it contain Colton's new birth certificate, but it also had the documentation that Colton was officially ours. It did not take us long to realize that the judge had signed the adoption on August 19, 2015. This was the same date ten years earlier that the Russian judge had signed Mikayla over to me. It felt like God tying Leeann and my relationship together with Colton and looping in Mikayla into one bright, beautiful bow. Now every year, we celebrate both of them on the same day. The day also reminds us of God's timing and the miraculous ways he orchestrated everything in our lives with such loving purpose.

CHAPTER 13

HOLY TOLEDO! A TREATMENT ARISES

OVER THE NEXT THREE YEARS, things were looking up for me. I had switched to a different hospital but still in Toledo and was the athletic trainer at nearby Springfield High School in Holland. I had a wonderful wife, two beautiful kids, a school, and a company—Mercy Health Systems—I felt at home with. However, it was beginning to get more difficult for me to stand for long periods of time or walk for long distances. If I did certain activities for long, not only would my knees get sore but my muscles also would begin to fatigue, altering my gait pattern, which made my knee issues worse. During football games, I needed to sit on a bench during timeouts or at quarter-breaks just to rest my legs. This was the first time in many years that I had started to feel like I was to the point that I may not be able to do this.

In the fall of 2017, Dr. Robert "Buzz" Heizelman decided to join me on the sidelines as team doctor because his son, Jacob, had transferred in from Central Catholic to Springfield and was on the team. Buzz had been my primary care physician since I started working for Mercy Health. Buzz had a sports medicine background and worked for Mercy Health too, which make it an easy choice for our team to put him with me on Friday nights at the football games. During our second home game, he approached me and said he noticed I was having difficulty walking. I had been trying so long to hide my struggles and blend in; he was the first person to notice. He said he would do some research and see if there was anything that could help.

I felt that night that this was my saving grace. I began to have some hope of a treatment for my condition. I had not been to a neurologist since the year after my diagnosis when I quit going for two reasons. One was that every time I went to the clinic, all they seemed to say was "see you in six months." The second reason was I had already made the decision to go against medical advice with my athletic training career, and I didn't want to have to justify that to them. A few times a year I received the SMA newsletter, but there was no new news in them about treatments plans, so at one point I quit reading.

A couple weeks after we had spoken, Buzz tagged me in an email he had sent to Ohio State University. A day later, a nurse for one of the neurologists who oversaw patients with SMA responded by email and said that a new FDA-approved drug, nusinersen, had been officially signed off on that past December (2016).

As with most pharmaceuticals, the drug had been in development for years. A year after my diagnosis, the neurologist in Indianapolis told me scientists had located and identified the gene that causes SMA, called the Survival Motor Neuron (SMN). Over two decades, scientists conducted numerous trials, testing variations of the drug.

I remembered Kevin had gone through some of those research trials one year in college. Some of the drugs he had no reaction to, but one Thanksgiving, one of the drugs had caused his hands to shake worse than they ever had. He would scoop up food with a serving spoon, but his hand shook so violently that before he could get it to his mouth, half of it would fall back onto the plate. I told myself that if nusinersen was that drug, I couldn't function or live like that and would probably not go through with the treatment.

While I waited to get in to see the neurologist, I gathered information about the drug, what it did, the treatment protocol, and how it was administered. I also contacted a drug representative case manager, Jason Braddock, who answered a lot of my questions. He told me that in order to be approved for this drug, I must have a deleted SMN1 gene and have at least one to three SMN2 genes present. These genes determine the extent and severity of a person's condition. Once that information was determined, the neurologist would put me through a round of tests, including a six-minute walk test and the same test I had taken when I was first diagnosed to assess my gross and fine motor skills. If I met the criteria and my insurance approved treatment, I would receive a loading dose, which consisted of four shots over a two-month period, with the first three shots every two weeks. Then I would proceed to the maintenance phase, where I would get one shot every four months. I asked about the side effects of hand tremors and was promised that the hand tremors I had at the time should lessen, and that reassured me.

Leeann and I headed to Columbus one afternoon to Wexner Medical Center and the Martha Morehouse Outpatient Care neurology clinic. The anticipation of what this new doctor might tell us raised my anxiety level. The last time I had even been to the neurologist for my condition was almost twenty-four years ago. I had a sense of the same eerie, dark feeling I had felt that day. When Dr. Bakri Elsheikh entered the room, I began to be nervous for the opposite reason. Was I too advanced to qualify? Had I hit all the blood work markers I needed to receive this treatment? These and other concerns raced through my mind.

We started with the history of the development of my condition. For this information, I actually had to call my mom and have Dr. Elsheikh ask her questions about my development as a child. My mom was more nervous than I was, and as she was answering him, I could hear her voice quiver. I contributed the information about not being fast and tripping a lot while playing sports. I shared that I attributed a lot of my symptoms at the time to my being lazy.

Then the doctor ran me through the gamut of testing to see how my body reacted to stress and physical pressure. My upper-body strength in my shoulders, biceps, and triceps was decent; however, my lower extremities were a different story. He tested my hip flexion by making me lift my knees one at a time while sitting on the edge of a table; I have always compensated by leaning to the side to be able to lift them. Then he tested my quadriceps (thigh) strength by making me kick each foot out in front of me from the table. That one I could do only by swinging my leg to get it to move forward. In another muscle test, he pressed down on my hands while I held my arms out in front of me. He did not have to apply much pressure before my arms collapsed. As a male, that didn't make me feel real dominant to be physically manipulated so easily by a man who was probably twenty years older than I was.

After he was finished, he explained what was next for me and how the injections would work. I already knew a lot of this procedure through talking with Jason. He had probably gotten though half his spiel when my wife interrupted him and asked, "So from what you have seen and through his tests, he will qualify to start treatment?" Dr. Elsheikh responded, "Yes, pending insurance approval. But we have not had issues getting approval from them so far, so from my standpoint, he qualifies to begin starting as soon as we can get him in." Leeann got teary-eyed with relief and excitement; I was feeling the same.

Dr. Elsheikh went on to explain that I might gain some of my strength over time, and the medicine would begin to slow down the progression of the disease. After twenty-five years of living with my condition, I felt like there was hope I could last longer with my job, be able to walk my daughter down the aisle when she got married someday, and continue shooting a basketball or throwing a baseball in the backyard with my son.

After three months of waiting, the day finally arrived for my first of four shots. Leeann, Colton, and I left at 5:30 in the morning, but I didn't get much sleep the night before anyway because I was so nervous about the procedure. After the doctor reviewed my X-rays and the blood work I had drawn a few days before, nurses prepped my back and located my L3–L4 vertebrae on the portable X-ray machine.

A needle was stuck into my spinal column and into my spinal cord so they could slowly allow my spinal fluid to drain out. Once enough was out, through the same needle, the drug was slowly administered straight into my spinal cord. All I needed to do was stay as still as possible. The only pain I felt was in numbing my skin. Once the needle was inserted, they said I would feel some pressure, but I didn't.

During this whole time, I looked at the X-ray tech and talked his ear off just to get my mind off what was going on in my back. As they continued, I could feel my palms sweating and tingling from the death grip I had on the table. In twenty minutes, we were done with shot number one. After lying down in a recovery room for an hour, I was able to leave with instructions I needed to lie flat for the next two days in order to reduce the side effects of spinal headaches. I was told the headaches should be gone after two days.

Not knowing how my body would react to the spinal infusion, we had decided we would be better off staying in Columbus that night so I could lie on my back as long as possible and see how much pain I was in before heading back to Toledo. I walked out to the car with no problems at all. Our plan was for me to lie flat in the back seat to be as comfortable as possible, but we had forgotten to move my son's car seat to the other side to make room for me. We had only a fifteen-minute drive back to the hotel, so I thought, *No worries, I'll be fine sitting up.*

After about ten minutes, a pressure headache came on, then worsened. Colton hadn't eaten lunch yet, so my wife decided to stop at McDonalds. By then, the headache was making me nauseous. We finally got to the hotel, and as soon as I lay down, mercifully, my headache went away.

I returned to work on day three, but I still was having headaches, although they were a little less intense. In the middle of football practice that day, however, I had to lie on the ground with my head on a lineman's pad to watch practice—but I stuck it out. Over the next two days, the pressure headaches went away when I was standing, and I only got headaches when I exerted myself or bent over to pick something up from the ground.

In the next twenty-eight days, I got the second and third shots. After each one, the headaches lasted longer. One day I was sitting in the training room at my computer doing some charting and I broke down crying. I thought to myself, *I don't know if I can do this feeling like this.* I prayed for God to give me a sign that this was what I was supposed to be doing to help my condition. The following day we had our first scrimmage at the high school. I was curious to see what would happen if I stood during the game. I made it through the entire game without taking a break, and even at halftime, I stood next to the fence at the stadium. This was the sign I needed, and it gave me the strength to continue with the shots.

Over the next month, I noticed a bigger difference in the weight room. I couldn't lift a ton more, but I was able to do a few more reps than I ever had. I also recovered from my workouts a little quicker. The biggest difference was that for the past five years, I could not work out and do yard work on the same day. Now I finally was able to do both and not be so fatigued.

CHAPTER 14

TRAINING FOR THE RACE OF MY LIFE

WORKING OUT WAS THE FIGHT I HAD FOUGHT for almost twenty-five years. I was told at the age of eighteen that I would not be able to go into a career I desperately wanted. So every day I went in the gym, it was my goal to make myself better and stronger. I had kept that focus for years. This is not to say I didn't have days where I just didn't want to go in. But every day, I dragged my butt in there and did my workout, even on the days I was coming down with a cold or wasn't feeling the greatest. You could find me at the gym at five in the morning sweating on the cardio machines or pushing a sled. It was who I was—a competitor.

Throughout my career, I had watched many winners: athletes making the winning bucket at the end of basketball games, quarterbacks marching their team down the field and scoring a winning, tennis players putting away opponents with wicked backhands. I loved watching those moments and more from the sidelines, encouraging and yelling at the athletes to do their best.

Before I started treatment, I worked a few years with Dave's Running Shop near Toledo, covering numerous events like their 5K and 10K fun runs and the Mercy Health Glass City Marathon. I was able to ride the course along with the athletes, as it was my job to make sure if someone was in any type of distress, I was there to take care of them. I treated a few people occasionally, but mainly I encouraged the runners as they competed.

The weekend after my final loading dose in October 2019, I was working a 5 km and 10 km race at Macqueen Orchards, enjoying seeing all the families with signs and hearing them cheer on their friends and family members. I had seen so much of this, but that day for some reason, I thought, *Why can't I do a race like this and cross the finish line just like all the other people—the normal people?* It reminded me of the class I took in graduate school at Ball State the first semester after I graduated when I was able to compete with the able-bodied individuals and the disabled body individuals. We were there for a purpose to not only stay active but also to achieve a task. I knew that I would not be able to run such a race but thought I could at least walk the course. This thought surprised, scared, and excited me, and I let it sink into my muscles and cells for more motivation in the gym.

A month later, the burning desire I had in me for the race was still there. I called Susan Haverland, a friend I had met through the

SMA community and someone who deals with people with SMA on a daily basis, and asked if she thought it would be okay for me to do a 5 km race. She immediately responded, "First, yes, as long as Dr. Elsheikh approves you, I think it would be a great idea. But Kurt, I was actually thinking about you this past weekend at an adventure I was in. I think you would be perfect for it." She explained she had just finished a 120-mile, three-day adventure, biking and kayaking from Key Largo to Key West in Florida. One of the contestants who finished the race with her was a young lady with a diagnosis of spina bifida, which is a birth defect where the spinal cord does not form properly, causing difficulty mainly in the lower extremities and reducing the ability to walk. Susan continued, "Kurt, with all the working out that you do, this would be a race that would totally fit you. On top of that, you can apply for a grant that would give you the opportunity to make the entire trip for free."

I thought at first, *Susan, I just want to do 3.1 miles, and you want me to do 120. Are you nuts?* My second thought was, *How cool! I totally want to try.*

I could not get off the phone fast enough with Susan that evening to look up more about this challenge. I went to *ProjectAthena.org* and looked up Florida Keys to Recovery Adventure. I scrolled through the pages and came to a video and immediately pushed play. It showed life-affirming scenes of women and men kayaking and biking in lush wilderness. Inspiring stories of Athenas and Zeuses unfolded on the site. They were mainly people who had had a medical setback and, as grant recipients, made their comeback by participating in one of the foundation's several adventures.

The story of a young lady in high school who had torn her ACL while playing field hockey stood out to me. After forty-three surgeries by the time she was twenty-one, she decided to have her leg amputated above the knee. She undertook the adventure because she wanted to get back her life as the athlete she used to be. The smile and joy in her eyes crossing that finish line broke my heart. I instantly thought, *That is me, and this comeback is exactly what I need.* I knew I had to become one of Project Athena's Zeuses.

I downloaded the application for the foundation's grant and explained why I wanted to be a part of this adventure. I waited for about a month then got a text that Louise Cooper, Athena's chief inspiration officer, would be calling me around eight that night to discuss my application. You know that feeling when you're anticipating something in the mail and you check it numerous times wishing It would arrive? Yes, that was me looking at my watch every fifteen to twenty minutes to see if the call was getting closer.

At eight on the dot, Louise called me from California. She asked me to tell her why this adventure would mean so much to me. I recounted my journey as an athlete, being diagnosed with SMA, and fighting to prove a physician wrong since the age of eighteen. I said I had given up sports and competitions for fear of getting hurt and not being able to maintain my strength. I went on to tell her about my shots and how much more energy I had, and how badly I wanted to cross a finish line. She said, "So you're ready for a breakthrough." I had never thought of it that way. "Yes, a breakthrough," I replied. She said, "Well, Kurt, we would like to offer you a grant for the Florida Keys to Recover Adventure the next year in November as one of our Zeuses." I was stunned. I had officially signed up for my first race EVER!

I remember a sermon one day that one of my pastors took from the book of Acts. The basis of the sermon was that God provides us with the building blocks and sets the foundation for our lives. It is that foundation that gives us the opportunity to see the beauty of life and feel gratitude for what he gives us. An example he used was when looking at a house, we don't see underneath it to what keeps the house standing, and only if we are building a new house and are able to see the huge hole in the ground when the foundation is laid, we never see that work. All we see is the beauty of the structure when it is finished.

A marathon runner or an Ironman triathlete does not just show up on race day and show everyone how fantastic an athlete they are to be able to finish a race. It takes many months of training and preparing their bodies to endure what they are going to produce on race day. Many times, this training is done on their own with no one around, and like the foundation of a house, it is not the most beautiful part, so it goes largely unseen. But the beautiful part of the house could not be built and come to exist or be admired without that foundation.

The message of the sermon that day was that in order to succeed in the end, you have to build a foundation for that beauty to come forth. I now saw that most of my life, what I had gone through was building the foundation for this next challenge. Perhaps that foundation even had to be partially knocked down to get me to where I was today. I knew at that point that I needed to start training to make sure that on the day of the adventure, about a year later, my body had the foundation to be able to conquer 120 miles.

Over the next several months, I ran the gamut of emotions and doubt. I was excited and told many of my athletes and coaches at school. Many responded, "That is so cool." But I also got a lot of "You're doing what?" The one person I was afraid to tell was my mom. I had mentioned to her as soon as I applied for the grant that

I wanted to do this race. Her first response was she didn't want me doing it because she was afraid of undoing any of the treatment I had been getting. Even after I told her my new neurologist said it would be an excellent thing to do, she was unsure about me participating. So the day I got the news I had received the grant, I didn't want to call her. I think it was the fear she might try to talk me out of doing something I knew I wanted to do.

I went through Christmas, Valentine's Day, and even Easter without saying anything to her about it. When we visited my parents for July 4th, my mom asked me, "You're not still doing that 120-mile thing, are you?" I almost puked. But I explained I was, and I was training correctly with PAF's help to build up the endurance to go the distance over the three days, and I would be in a group the entire time on the trip. She seemed to be more at ease, and her last words to me were, "Just don't get hurt."

My training was definitely not all on my own. The thing about the PAF is that the participants are from all over the United States and even overseas. So in order to ensure proper training, we were given an app that had workouts starting four months before our adventure and leading up to the day of the race. As each day appeared on the training plan, we would log the number of hours or miles completed for each workout. Some were even timed workouts we would try to complete under or in a certain time to ensure pacing and how fast we were going.

Throughout the training, I often thought of my mom's words: "Don't get hurt." Our coach, Amanda Webb, was supportive and always on-call, so I am sure by the end of training, she was glad the race was near, so she wouldn't get another email from me about it. I stuck to the plan closely in the four months prior to the race.

I always liked to look ahead in my training plan at what I'd be doing and what benchmarks I'd need to hit in order for PAF to give us the clearance and say we were ready to complete the journey. These benchmarks were spaced to build us up to passing the final requirements and ensuring we were properly trained to complete the adventure in Florida. I saw that my last requirement for the bike was thirty miles in three hours. This was a concern for me. When I began a ride, I averaged between eight and nine mph, but as I pedaled more miles, I would slow down to six and seven. So I set my mind to getting up to ten miles per hour and sustaining that pace for three hours. Doubt crept in, and I questioned whether I could do enough for the foundation to allow me to go.

Before my training, I talked to Bobblyn Long about my race and my training. Bobblyn was the mother of two of the athletes I was currently closely working with at Springfield High School. Her son was an outstanding lineman and probably the biggest, strongest kid I ever worked with. Her daughter was also an amazing softball player and volleyball player. When I told Bobblyn about my event, she said she would go riding with me. For my longer rides, I would call her and her friend Donny to go with me. Having someone with me pushed me to go faster than I ever had, and I understood how valuable it was for teammates to push each other to go beyond what they felt was possible. Having that support throughout training propelled me to achieve the goals I had set, including keeping up with the pace I would need for the final requirements.

On the day of the final requirements for participating, I set out with one goal in mind—to come in below three hours for the thirty miles. The day was a beautiful sunshiny one with barely any wind. I started off at a slower pace, but within a few miles, my legs kicked in and began to get ahead of the necessary pace. In the last few miles, however, I felt myself slowing down. I remembered Bobblyn telling me in our rides, "We are almost there; you are so close. Pick it up a just a little bit and you will hit your mark." I thought to myself, "This is the time where I'll either put up or shut up." My phone app spit out the mileage and the time at each mile. I pedaled and watched as it said twenty-seven miles, then twenty-eight, twenty-nine, and finally thirty with a time of 2:59. I had done it! I had completed the final requirement and aced the day's goal.

I could not wait to plug those numbers into my log and send it to Coach Amanda. The next day she sent me an email that said, "Congrats, Kurt, you have completed the final requirement. This officially qualifies you to join the race in the Florida Keys."

It reminded me of people who have to qualify for the Boston Marathon every year. Everyone who gets invited to Boston has to qualify before they are allowed to run, and every year the organizers set a time that participants must at least come close to to even be considered. Hopeful runners complete a race within the guidelines, then they just have to wait for the letter that lets them know if they qualified for that prestigious race. This was my Boston Marathon qualification and my acceptance to participate in an athletic event. Did I say athletic event? Yes, I did.

Even after qualifying, the months leading up to the Keys to Recovery event were nerve-racking. I had completed all the training requirements but still felt as if it wasn't enough. Even when I was supposed to be tapering off my workouts so my body could heal before the event, I continued to lift as often as I had done for the past twenty-five years. My thought was that if I didn't continue to lift, I would lose the strength I had worked so hard to build—and I was terrified of that happening.

During the last month of training, I walked into the gym one day ready to start my normal routine on the bench. I was thinking about how far I had come and how my trip to the Keys was inching ever closer. I felt this weird, anxious rumbling in my body. I knew it was a feeling of excitement, but it was unusual. I approached one of the personal trainers and explained what I was feeling, and he said, "Kurt, you're getting butterflies. Perfectly normal."

That struck me. Butterflies? I had heard athletes talk about the feeling they sometimes got before a big event, and it reminded me of the fight-or-flight rush we get when we are put in a dangerous situation. For me, the butterflies were a sign my body was getting pumped up for what it knew was coming.

CHAPTER 15

ARRIVING IN
THE KEYS

ALTHOUGH THE PROJECT ATHENA EVENT wasn't until mid-November, I started packing my bags in late October. I wanted to make sure I could fit all the required gear in the single bag I was allowed. Plus, it calmed my anxiety about forgetting something. I must have packed, unpacked, and repacked that bag at least four times. It was surely nervousness not necessity, but at least it succeeded in distracting my brain.

When the day to leave finally arrived, my father-in-law dropped me at the airport for the early morning flight that would put me in Ft. Lauderdale midday. I was tired when I landed, so I went straight to our hotel, and I fell asleep early but was jolted awake just after midnight. In response to some not-so-subtle knocking, I opened the door to find a short, spunky Filipino man carrying a giant duffle bag. My midnight impression was that this guy was either a true night owl or he had downed one too many espressos. Turned out, he was just an incredible, life-loving, bundle of exhilaration at all times of the day. This was my introduction to Ernie Villanueva, one of the Project Athena Trail Angels.

Athena Trail Angels are a special group of individuals who make the adventure experience possible. There are two groups of angels. One group are the individuals who go along on the adventure side-by-side with the participants, playing many roles, first as encouraging cheerleader when it seems someone is struggling. They can use words or give the occasional push from behind on the bike, or more rarely, attach a towline to a kayak in the ocean. They also are repairers in case a bike breaks down or a tire blows or they need to fix a boat so it turns properly in the ocean.

The other group of angels are the road crew (Ernie was in this group). These are the people who move things from one stopping point to the other, so that when we complete each leg, we have our gear to change for the next activity and some well-deserved lunches, snacks, and the occasional water refueling. In case something happens on the adventure with one of the participants or crew, these angels are available to pick them up.

Right behind Ernie that night came my roommate, Jeff Willis. Our stories were similar in that we were both battling degenerative diseases, but we were fighting our battles on very different fronts. Jeff's body was in great shape, but his vision was fading fast and eventually would be gone all together.

Jeff suffers from retinitis pigmentosa which is a form of cone-rod dystrophy. Only one in 4,000 people are affected by this rare

condition. When Jeff was four, he started noticing it was getting difficult for him to see at night. In high school while playing his favorite
sport of football, he experienced changes in his peripheral vision. Jeff
has slowly progressed to where the rods' photoreceptors are failing,
and his peripheral vision has narrowed. Jeff was diagnosed as legally
blind in 2007 but was partially sighted, meaning he could see only
certain things but would be very limited at night.

While living in Visalia, California, Jeff learned about Project
Athena through the Valley Center for the Blind in Fresno. He had
applied, wanting to show to his kids, family, and friends that he could
do anything they can do. I told him the adventure was probably more
than any normal-bodied person would ever want to do—and maybe
they were just a little smarter than we were.

I wasn't entirely sure how to assist a roommate with diminished
sight, but I settled on the idea that he, like me, would want to be
treated like any other person. Regardless of how well our various
body parts were functioning, the bottom line was that we were both
Zeuses ready to embark on a grand adventure and flip our setbacks
into comebacks.

The next morning, we met a few other early arrivers for breakfast. At the hotel buffet, Jeff and I were joined by Sarah Harris and
Chenier Derrick, a pair of blind best friends, with Barnaby the
guide dog leading the way. Pia Guerrin, a purple-haired Swedish
Virginian, and Megan Lane, the tag-along photographer also were
there. Chenier and Sarah were participants on PAF's Harbor to
Harbor trek off the San Diego coast a few years earlier.

Sarah was thirty-six in November 2002, when she was T-boned
by a car just half a block from her apartment. "It was at that moment,"
Sarah says, "my world plunged into darkness." After hours of surgery,

Sarah began the process of dealing with being permanently blind. Chenier was in and out of the hospital with glaucoma from birth until the age of thirteen. Barney, a golden Labrador retriever, was Chenier's guide dog. Chenier and Sarah were friends in Fresno; he saw Sarah do the PAF Cove to Harbor Marathon and wanted to try that one. Both of them decided to become a God/Goddess (fund raisers) and try the Florida Keys Adventure together.

Once we were all fed and watered up, we found a van to take us to the airport to meet up with the crew and other participants once we arrived back at the airport. I finally got to see a familiar face, Susan Haverland, the woman who had sparked my interest in all this. Knowing another person made me more comfortable, but my nerves remained frayed. For the ride to Key Largo, I sat next to Eric Kulikowski and Marianne Kuga, another God and Goddess. I would later realize that these two and many of the others on the trip had raised a certain amount of money, not only for themselves to be able to do this adventure but also to help fund the comebacks for others. Marianne was a member of the Big Speak organization, through which Athena founder Robyn Benincasa did a majority of her speaking engagements. Eric was a longtime God with Project Athena, going on many trips over the years.

Everyone was asking everyone else about what led them to Project Athena, so I found myself sharing my entire story. As I was telling it, I kept thinking, "These people can't be that interested in me." But those around me, including Robyn in the driver's seat, listened intently. This was actually the first time I truly opened up and shared my entire story without being asked about it first. It was a surprisingly comfortable conversation. I am still amazed at how quickly this group of strangers embraced each other and became a family. The unconditional acceptance and interest I experienced in that van set the tone for the entire experience.

We pulled into the campground near a national park. It was beautiful driving amid the trees and coming around a bend to see the inlet where we would be setting off in our kayaks the next morning and heading out into the Atlantic Ocean. We continued into the park and made it to our campsite, and we all got out to receive our gear and started setting up our tents. For some reason I ended up getting a tent all to myself, which I was fine with because I did not want to wake anyone during one of the number of times I get up in the night.

After tents were pitched, we all walked to a picnic site where they had dinner ready for us—pizza, pasta, and salad. I knew with my stomach, since I was not used to pizza, I should not eat the pizza. The next day, I could have Montezuma's revenge hit me while in a kayak with no restroom in the middle of the ocean. I stuck with some plain pasta and a salad, and it was an excellent choice.

Robyn introduced her crew of trail angels, and we finally got to know who the angels were and what they did. Then everyone else started to introduce themselves. Some were there from BigSpeak; others were there to honor family members or friends who had died of cancer by being a fund raiser and helping others achieve their dreams. The person who stood out to me the most during her introduction was Brittney Voss. She was a Minnesota girl who had just passed one year of being cancer-free. I thought of how exciting that would be to have beaten cancer and to celebrate that victory by going on this adventure.

After introductions, we headed back to the campsite to make sure our stuff was packed and ready to go in the morning. I think I repacked that transition bag probably five times to make sure I had everything I needed. I fell asleep by 9:30 but then woke up around 1:30 and just could not go back to sleep. I was hyper aware of the uncertainty of what I was embarking on.

Did I train enough? Was my body going to be able to handle the stress put on it? Was I going to be able to complete at least one day? What will happen if I capsize in the ocean? Will I be able to get back into the kayak? Then on top of all of that, my mom's concern came forward, Will I get hurt? And if I do, how much will it set me back from being able to do the job I have fought so hard to do for the past twenty-five years?

I would get my answers over the next three days as I traveled by bike and kayak—forty miles a day along the Atlantic coastline on one side and the Gulf of Mexico on the other—from Key Largo to the southernmost place you can travel to in the continental United States, the tip of Key West.

CHAPTER 16

DAY ONE

EVENTUALLY IT WAS TIME for me to get up and get going. We ate breakfast then made our way down to the dock area around 7 a.m. We gathered together before we went to pick out our kayaks, oars, and life vests, and to listen to Robyn's first morning sermon.

Here's what she had to say:

Why We're Here

Why we're here . . .

We're here to remember the people who can't be.

To share this beautiful place with them and to let our spirit soar with theirs.

We are here to celebrate our friends who have been so close to the edge, physically, spiritually, emotionally, but who are still standing here with us today, strong and beautiful and full of life.

We are here to enjoy being HERE, now, in this place, in this moment, and to appreciate our ABILITY to take each and every paddle stroke, feel each and every little ache, and to share this journey with the very cool people who surround us.

We are here to give of ourselves. To help, to be helped, to feed, to be fed, to limp, and to laugh, and to be one another's Goddess or God when the going gets tough. You will remember what happens today for the rest of your life: The smiles, the unspoken sister—and brotherhood—and the feeling that you have met friends you may well have for life. Rushing through this day is like getting to the bottom of a bowl of ice cream as fast as you can. Lick the spoon of this day, my friends! The joy is in the journey, the friendship, the stories, the ocean, the sky, the moment.

We're here because we want to help future Athenas and Zeuses overcome their setbacks and live their dreams. Your efforts will change many people's lives, make them stronger, and help them find the adventurous, capable, and confident girl or guy inside who can once again see a world of possibilities versus a world of question marks, doctor's offices, and hopelessness.

And last but not least, we're here to celebrate the success of every single person in this circle of luuuuv—the fact that we made it to Key Largo after months and months of training and fundraising. The fact that you had the chutzpah to believe this adventure was possible, and the fact that on Saturday night, you will be one of the very few people on Earth who has ridden, paddled, and run 120-ish miles from Key Largo to Key West! Can I get an amen, sistahs and brothahs?! Our team is so proud of and honored by each and every one of you before you even put your kayak into the beautiful blue water of the Atlantic Ocean. Thank you for sharing in this mission with us and each other and for embracing it with all of your heart and soul.

Let's go together now and embrace this day, and love being alive, and remember that we're not only "taking" an adventure, we're "giving" an adventure ... to ourselves, the friends who believed in us, and to the other women (and men) out there whose lives will forever be changed because you gave your sweat, blisters, aching shoulders, tired legs, and laughter to them today.

As Robyn was reading her speech, I took in every word she said about this journey, undertaken in earnest four months ago that had brought us to this, the start of the adventure. Besides the dread of soreness and floppy legs, the thing that stood out to me in that speech was the fact that over the next three days I would never forget this moment or what I was about to accomplish, and it was something only a few others had done. This was not like any of the 5 km races or 10 km races or marathons, where I was there riding on my bike as the runners crossed the finish line. No, this was going to be 120 miles, and I was going to experience it as a competitor. I was excited to jump into the kayaks and get started!

Robyn paired us newbie paddlers with people who were experienced, and weak with strong paddlers, to try to make everything as even as possible so we would all stay together. I was excited that for the first day, I was matched with Susan. We picked out our kayak and headed out. We were in a long inlet flowing out to the ocean, but halfway out, we realized we could not get our rudder to steer straight. We headed back to shore and eventually were pulled over by Blain Reeves, "The Reaper," who told us he could fix it.

Reaper was a battalion operations officer in the US Army during the 2003 Iraq War. His designation of The Reaper derived from The Grim Reaper and meant you were toward the back of the pack. As in life, you wanted to avoid the reaper, but Blain's job was probably the most special because, as he would explain later to me, "The back is where all the magic happens." His job was to keep the people at the back of the pack together with the rest of the group, and if there were any breakdowns on the bikes or kayaks, he was there to help fix them. He was also there to help those that might be slower or might have hit a wall along the journey to keep up with the rest of the pack. After a few adjustments to our rudder, we were back on track.

By now, the rest of the twenty-five members of the group had made headway toward the ocean. Blain had another paddler with him but decided to make us a four-person kayak by attaching a towline. Robyn explained this version of a towline perfectly:

In her adventure racing days, they would trek hundreds of miles. Certain people had strengths on one section but would be weaker on the other legs. She said this meant everyone would suffer equally overall. That is how they came up with towlines. Why should you have to wait for the slowest person, when you could just bring them with you at your pace? Once we got our towline connected to Superman Blain, we flew along with him up the channel to the ocean.

Funny thing about that towline. I did not realize what had happened until a few months later when I saw the pictures Megan (the photographer) took of us being towed. I had to look closely but could see I was paddling hard to keep us up with Blain. Susan, however, was reclining with her oar lying across the cockpit of the kayak. She looked like she was rummaging through her bag searching for a mimosa or something while Blain and I were madly paddling to get us back to the group. (Sorry, Susan; it's my book and I can call it as I saw it.) But eventually we caught up to the group waiting for us out in the ocean. It was such a beautiful sight of the sun on the fairly calm water, which was a blessing. Once we reached the group, we got a little bit of a breather before unclipping the towline and heading down the coast of southern Florida.

The last time I was even near the Keys was with my parents when I was around eight or nine. I remember going snorkeling and being able to see the coral reefs and the small fish and female sharks. And I remember how clear the water was. Now, in the kayak I got to see again that sparkling clear blue water. We were probably a half-mile away from the shore but could see the seaweed beds spreading out on the white sand bottom of the ocean, which was no deeper than eight feet where we were. As we looked out toward the ocean, it was nothing but clear skies and sun.

About halfway through the ride, I saw something cresting in the distance. I had to take a second glance then shouted, "Look! Two sets of dolphins." The pairs came over the horizon and were within twenty yards from a few of the kayaks. They followed us for a good twenty minutes before swimming off. Sarah, who was on her third PAF adventure and first one to the Keys, said she was able to hear them splash and make sounds. I appreciated how cool it was that we all experienced the dolphins in our own ways, with different senses.

After 11.5 miles, we made it to our first transition point—arriving on shore to the cheers from the trail crew. I was thrilled I had made it through the first leg of the day, no sharks, no tipping into the ocean. My arms were a little sore because it had taken me half the ride to figure out that I needed to use my back and my core instead of my biceps when pulling my oars through the water. I found my transition bag and took it to the bathroom to change into my biking stuff. As I walked into the bathroom, I saw Ernie helping Chenier with his gear. Ernie gave me some invaluable advice: "Make sure that you clean everything 'down there' of all the salt." Even though he was telling this to all the men and women, I'm sure there was someone on a previous trip who did not do this and had issues. So I made sure I was salt-free everywhere before I put on my bike gear.

I rushed over to where the bikes were so I was able to get a bike that would fit me. Because I am so much weaker when my knees are bent, I wanted a bike where I could raise the seat high enough so that I could extend my knees. When I finally got my bike, I think I had taken up twenty-five minutes of our allotted thirty minutes just getting my tires blown up and my handlebars fixed. This left me a quick five minutes to eat before hitting the road for a twenty-eight-mile ride. I noticed early on that pedaling my bike was a little bit harder than I had expected. I thought maybe it was just because it was a different bike and had only seven gears from what I could see.

I rode between the middle and the end of the pack, so I got to know a lot of the participants and crew. When I slipped to the back of the group, three of the crew members riding their own bikes would put a hand on my back and push me to pick up speed. One of this crew was Jack, who was on a tandem bike with Jeff, my roommate with the blindness. Jack was pulling double-duty pushing me and trying to balance his bike with Jeff on the back. The crew did this with numerous people along the path.

We made stops along our ride, not only to break up the twenty-eight miles but also to see some of the sights of the Keys. At one stop, the place was packed with cars, and I noticed many people on road bikes who seemed to be doing a race. We also noticed a storm coming in the distance, so we got back on the road hoping to beat the storm. At about mile twenty-two, a light rain turned to a downpour in just a matter of minutes. We experienced a Forrest Gump kind of rain: sideways rain, spitting rain, fat rain, even rain that seemed to come from the ground. To say we were drenched was an understatement. It felt like we had jumped into a pool with all our bike gear on, as we slogged through the hard rain for the next three or four miles.

Coming out of that storm, we were soaked, and all we wanted to do was get to our stopping point and get out of our wet clothes into dry ones. I had noticed I had two other gear rings but still could not figure out how to access them on my handlebars. After the storm, of course, I realized that the left handlebar turned to access more gears. I had been riding in third gear for the first twenty-five miles that day! At that point I was tired of pedaling and was at the back of the pack.

As usual, I found myself being pushed again by the crew. But this time, Jack pulled up behind me, and instead of grabbing my shirt as he had the previous times, he just put his hand on my back.

Before I knew it, the bottom part of my damp shirt got wrapped on his handlebars. Jack's voice rose in fear as his bicycle wheels started to swivel. I felt the bike starting to fall. Then his hands let go of my back and I felt something pushing me away from Jack and out of the way. Behind me I could hear Jack and Jeff's bike hit the ground. My first thought was, "Please, don't let them be hurt because of me." I didn't want to look back and see what had happened, but I needed to because they might be in need of my help. I saw they were in the process of trying to get the bike off their bodies. I walked back to them and saw the road rash on their faces, legs, and arms. Jack was moving pretty smoothly, but Jeff was still lying on the ground as if in shock. Jack and I asked Jeff what was hurt. Jeff said, "My legs and lower body just have a burning feeling from the scrapes, but my thumb really hurts. I think it might be broken."

Breaking something was the one thing I had always feared for myself, so Jeff's words sent chills down my spine. For so many years I was told not to break anything or it might set me back to the point that I might not be able to walk. Jack was a paramedic and nurse, so he began taking off Jeff's glove. As soon as he did, I instantly saw what was wrong. When he fell, Jeff had put his hand out, bending his thumb backward and dislocating it at the joint. Jack grabbed the thumb and pulled, setting it back in place. After they got the scrapes cleaned up and the splint put on, Blain and Jack helped Jeff stand up. They told me and another participant we should go ahead and catch up to the group, which we were able to do in just a few minutes.

It was inspiring when they eventually caught up with us, and we made it to our stop for the night together. I heard later that Jack had told Jeff he had two options. One was to get the van to come pick them up and drive him to where we were stopping, which would have been totally fine. Or they could get back on the bike and finish the darn thing. Of course, Jeff said, "Let's finish."

That night at dinner we celebrated the first day's success and heard that the big talk of the day was Jeff pushing through adversity to do what he had to do to finish. I was able to see the road rash on Jack and Jeff's faces and legs and could relate to that feeling from the numerous times my legs had given out and I had scraped them and ripped plenty of pants. Even though I was so tired, I kept replaying what had happened with Jack and Jeff. This was the first time during the trip that I felt afraid of falling off the bike.

Though I was excited I had made it through one-third of the trip, I still had two more days left. My saving graces were that we had a dryer to dry my clothes, a very warm shower to warm me up, and a plush pillow-top bed to sleep in that night.

Me and Susan Haverland getting paired up in the kayak on day one. I was so glad to have her not only in my life but also in my kayak on my first time entering the Atlantic Ocean.

One of the two sets of porpoises that crested in the distance just
yards from our kayaks in the middle of the Atlantic Ocean.

After getting our rudder fixed and "Reaper" putting a tow
line on our boat to catch us up to the rest of the group.
Susan rummaging through her bag for a mimosa while
the other three of us try to catch up with the group.

Me and Susan Haverland just chilling in
the middle of the Atlantic Ocean.

Jeff and Jack on the tandem bike behind me on day
one. Maybe an hour before my shirt got caught on
their handle bars as Jack was pushing me.

CHAPTER 17

DAY TWO

I WOKE UP ON DAY TWO after another mediocre sleep, still running the scenario with Jeff in my mind. I felt so bad that it was my shirt that had caused Jack's handlebars to go out of control and send them both crashing. I was grateful I had been able to ride out of that situation without a scar on my body—but for them to have been hurt left a scar in my mind. It was hard to turn my focus back to the race, but I had to. It wasn't just day two on the 2019 Project Athena Keys to Recovery Adventure; it was my forty-fourth birthday. I was concentrating more on making it just another day to get through while searching in the back of my mind for some significance to being on the ride on my birthday, so I wasn't expecting anything from any of the people I was with. But as soon I showed up at breakfast across the parking lot from our hotel, it took maybe two minutes before Zina

Mercil yelled out, "Happy Birthday, Kurt!" I answered my thanks with a smirky smile. I somewhat sheepishly received the wave of happy birthdays from everyone until they subsided, and I gratefully turned to getting our work done and getting through day two.

After breakfast, Robyn delivered our day two sermon:

Athena Ceremony: Who Is an Athena?

We're here to honor our awesome and courageous Athenas and Zeuses on their journey from survivor to adventurer and inspiration for all of us. The Keys to Recovery is a new beginning for them. It's a symbol of having made it through that tunnel of darkness and emerged into the light . . . of not just having their old life back but of enjoying the small gifts and silver lining their setback has given them in the form of an even more enlightened life with a renewed sense of purpose and grace, and a strong desire to not only become better and stronger for themselves but for everyone around them. What we hear so often from our Athenas and Zeuses is that they want to GIVE back what so many have given to them during their struggles and setbacks. THIS is what it means to be an Athena/Zeus—an Athena is never thinking "poor me," and an Athena/Zeus has no regrets; an Athena/Zeus appreciates every moment she or he has and wants to bring others to the light with them. An Athena/Zeus is grateful beyond measure for how beautiful the day is, how beautiful the world is. An Athena/Zeus reaches out to others, takes their hand, and shows them the way. Athena is the Goddess of Wisdom and War. Isn't it amazing how these wars with our bodies and with our setbacks have given us so much wisdom?

And that is what our mission here as a team on the Keys to Recovery Adventure is all about—Goddesses, Gods, Athenas, and Zeuses alike! Taking that wisdom everyone in this circle has earned and sharing it with one another on our quest for Key West! Today we will once again symbolically and literally push, pull, tug, tow, and inspire each other every paddle and pedal of the way, because together we are better than any of us can be alone.

This hit me to the core—I, too, was searching for the wisdom and purpose in my setback and wanting to carry it forward to others. I had spent the first six to seven years of my life after the diagnosis in a dark tunnel, not knowing the purpose behind why my condition was happening to me. I had spent the first part of that period just trying to stay afloat and accomplish a goal of proving a physician wrong. That changed once I realized my purpose was to show people that even with a disability or disadvantage in life, if you put your mind to it, you can accomplish anything. Hearing Robyn confirm that purpose and include me with these other brave, wonderful people meant the world to me.

After Robyn was finished, she asked Eric Kulikowski (I always called him the Pittsburgh guy) to tell his story of the "Be Brave" coin we received that day. Eric was a CrossFit gym owner from that city, who was participating in his seventh Keys to Recovery event the year I met him. He had applied for this event six years earlier after being at one of Robyn's speaking engagements he attended. Eric's wife,

Cindy, was diagnosed with stage 2 cancer in 2009—a mastectomy and hormone replacement therapy cancer didn't stop it from returning in 2014. That year, Cindy, as an Athena, would complete her first adventure with the Project Athena Foundation with her husband by her side. Cindy and Eric would return to Florida both as a God and Goddess just as Cindy had started chemotherapy six weeks earlier.

After the last night of the adventure in 2014, everyone could notice how frail she was, but never knew what Cindy was actually going through. Before dinner that night, Eric had approached Robyn to let her know about the situation and that some of her hair had fallen out in the shower that night. When they returned from the Keys, her health deteriorated and, eventually, four short months later, she gained her angel wings and went to see her maker. She was finally free of cancer but no longer with Eric.

Eric described how every day she went to chemo, she would take her coin stamped with "Be Brave" on it, along with wearing her PAF T-shirt, with her as a reminder she could accomplish anything as long as she kept those two simple words with her, and that coin reminded her of who she was, a Project Athena Finisher. The day her body was laid to rest, Eric placed her "Be Brave" coin beside her. PAF had a ritual of giving participants their own "Be Brave" coins as inspiration and comfort—symbols that they are brave in more ways than they can believe. Cindy had held hers the whole way through her treatments. As I looked down at the coin in my hand, I felt the presence of God urging us on just as Cindy did with hers.

We began day two on the bike after that emotional send-off that Eric gave us. At least I now knew I had fourteen extra gears on my bike—and I was going to need every last one of them today even though at the time I really didn't know what that day would bring for me. The rainstorm of day one brought a fifteen mph headwind on day two, which was made more problematic by the literal bridges we had to cross, seemingly every half a mile. These were no picturesque, short structures but long, two-lane concrete highways shared with cars and trucks. My legs had taken a little bit to awaken that morning, but eventually we made it to our stop after ten miles to get a snack and get back into the kayaks.

This time I was paired up with Nicole Carter. A native of Florida, she told me as we paddled that she had been able to do one of her training runs near a sanctuary of beluga whales. The water at the beginning was semi-calm with some waves but none that were any bigger than the day before. Robyn gathered us together in the ocean about a third of the way through our ten-mile trip to give us instructions for the next section of the bay area we were approaching. This was the first time on the trip we had done this, other than the times we gathered so everyone could catch up with each other. She said the area we were entering had produced some major waves in the past, and with the wind blowing out from the bay, the waves might be more intense than usual. She then explained how to navigate through them. "If you feel like you are going to roll," she said, "slap the top of the wave you are tipping toward with your oar to help balance the kayak."

Rather than reassure me, this instruction triggered one of my biggest pre-race fears—the fear of falling out of the kayak into the ocean. In training, I had worked hard on my kayaking after receiving the grant to ensure I'd make it through the adventure. I had even bought a blow-up kayak so I could participate in and complete a safety and water rescue course. Before the class, I did not know how to get back into the kayak if something happened, and getting dumped into the ocean was still a big fear for me.

That class had started out showing us how to manage the oars and how to paddle—all while on land. We had learned how to go forward then how to turn the kayak each direction and how to stop it. The instructor was able to demonstrate these techniques on land then eventually in the water. The instructors also demonstrated the different ways of getting out of and back into the kayak from the water. Each approach had its own difficulty level along with ways that matched someone's strengths or compensated their weaknesses. I had brought my blow-up kayak to class, but they let me use one of their single kayaks since that was what I would use in the Keys. When we finally pulled into the water, it felt awesome to be able to use a normal kayak, not only because it was more stable than my blow-up but also because it was much faster. Once we got out into a deeper part of the lake, the instructors went over all the different ways of getting out of the boat and getting back in. As soon as the instructor mentioned getting out of the kayak, my heart rate and anxiety rose.

We had split off into groups, and after one of my group members had successfully gotten out and then back in the kayak, I was next. With my heart racing, I was able to pull myself out of the cockpit and into the water fairly easily. All of the techniques involved us working with another boat to help stabilize each other's boats while the swimmer—me, in this case—got back in.

The first approach I tried was pulling myself up over the front (or bow) of the kayak. This maneuver required me to flutter-kick my feet fast enough to propel me out of the water, and though my upper body had a decent amount of strength, I had lost strength over the years before treatment and I was unable to accomplish this. The next few ways were equally hard, including using a rope ladder and pushing my butt out of the water with my legs; they were equally failed attempts because I could not extend my legs straight enough to lift myself up. Eventually, we had utilized a flotation device that looked like an air bladder, which we attached to the end of my oar. We then placed the oar where half of it was across both kayaks. I was able to place my foot on top of the flotation device and the oar, and after what seemed like twenty minutes of effort, I was finally back in my boat, too tired to even feel relief.

Once everyone had practiced, we all had a second opportunity to try it again. This time I instantly went to the technique I'd been successful with. However, I was so exhausted from the first attempts, I just did not have the strength to get back in the boat, so the instructor did a scoop technique where she put my boat partly underwater, and I got into it as she pulled the boat back over to the upright position. I had to pump the water out of the kayak shell that was halfway filled with water, but I was in. The one thing I kept thinking was, Would I be able to get back in the boat in the wavy ocean after rowing for a few hours if I had an emergency?

That experience was in the back of my mind as we entered the bay and the waves started to rise higher. All I could think of was, *Please do not tip over and get dumped into this choppy water*, and I questioned again if I would be able to get back in Nicole's and my boat with my barely practiced training technique and with the waves being so rough. Things got worse, but I continued to paddle and just hoped Nicole and I could get to the other side. Every so often, a motorized fishing boat would come across our bow and cause a wake in the other direction of the waves we were hitting, making our kayak feel like it was in a washing machine. The waves' unpredictability made forward progress even more difficult.

Halfway through, out of the corner of my eye, I noticed a few of the other kayaks turning around toward Robyn's boat and Chenier's boat, and I saw it tip over. I thought, *If Robyn, the three-times world record holder in the kayak and stand-up paddling can go over, how am I still able to stay up?* Nicole and I were able to slow down but keep upright, and Robyn and Chenier were able to get back into their kayak.

About thirty minutes later, Eric also tipped over in his single kayak. Though we were closer, a couple of the other kayaks behind us were able to get to him quicker, so we stayed our course, and eventually, after about ninety minutes of struggling through the high waves, we finally hit the other side of the bay where the water was much calmer. Once everyone got through, we paddled maybe another twenty minutes to where the road crew was waiting with our lunch. I had never wanted to get out of anything more in my life than I did that kayak.

After a good shower and a lunch, we were off on the third leg of our journey. This last part of the day was about eighteen miles and then we'd be done for the day; however, this leg would include crossing the dreaded Seven Mile Bridge. Robyn again gave us instructions before we started. She said we would not stop on the bridge at all, only on the other side to catch up with each other, and she gave us a few pointers for navigating this span of two-lane highway with very narrow bike lanes. She said, "As you go over the bridge, do not stop! If a bike breaks down or something goes wrong, pull over as close to the guard barriers as you can to allow the people behind you to pass." I remembered going over the bridge when I was about nine or ten on a family vacation to Key West. It was a long, narrow bridge flanked on both sides by the expanse of the ocean. I had talked about riding over that bridge since I'd been accepted. But now that I knew it was here, I was more than a little nervous than I had been the whole trip.

As we were made our way through town, we still battled a constant fifteen mph headwind. Reaper and Danny (Robyn's nephew) were next to me, pushing me to keep me up with the group. Every time I felt their hands on my back nudging me forward, I tightened my death grip on my bike remembering what had happened the day before with Jeff and Jack and anticipating the long bridge ahead.

Eventually, I saw it right in front of me. I was the last person, besides Danny and Reaper, so I got to watch everyone start their way over the bridge. On previous bridges, we had a fairly generous path or a sidewalk to ride on. On this one, all we had to ride on was a four-foot-wide shoulder running along the right side of the two-lane road of traffic going at least fifty-five miles an hour over the bridge. On the road, cars, SUVs, and pickup trucks, bulky dump trucks, large box trucks, and the occasional semi whipped by us with only the white line between us. To our right was a five-foot-high, thick concrete barrier protecting us from what I would say was a forty-foot drop into the deep waters of the Gulf of Mexico; the Atlantic Ocean was across the road on the left.

As I crossed over the last patch of land, I looked ahead to see if I could see our destination at the end of the bridge. The day was partly cloudy, which caused a little bit of a haze in the distance. I peered through my sunglasses, scouring for the land on the other side. As hard as I looked across the seven-mile span, I could not see any land on the horizon.

I remembered my mantra for all the training I had done over the prior four months: Just put your head down and keep pedaling. Questions swirled in my head: What was I thinking to do this?

Would I survive? Why am I here? What if I fail on my birthday? I fought with all my inner strength to banish these doubts and return to my mantra and keep moving.

The wind continued to bat us in the face at fifteen mph, making each stroke of the pedal that much harder. I felt like a circus performer riding on a tightrope without a net, high above the water in a wind tunnel surrounded by speeding vehicles. I remembered from numerous rides against headwinds that battling the wind was going to slow me down. The other riders in front of me were also feeling this and had their own issues, but they did not have a neurological condition that depleted their strength as they rode like I did. After what felt like four miles, but was probably only the first one, I really wanted to stop and take a break. But I knew we were on a road with nowhere to safely stop, and everyone ahead was still riding. Michelle Marlborough was one of those riders.

Michelle was chief products officer for a healthcare research firm in New York who had been told by one of her friends who had completed other Project Athena events to come and do this adventure with him. I kept looking ahead at Michelle, and I could see from her body language that she was struggling as much as I was. Danny and Reaper were bouncing back and forth between Michelle and me, pushing us both to try to speed up our pace, as they saw we were falling behind. I tried my best to pedal as hard as I could, so they didn't need to push me.

The Reaper was stronger than Danny, not only in body size but also in brute strength from all the bike and adventure races he had participated in over his career. So I felt bad for Danny, because even though he continued to be encouraging, each time he came to push me, I could feel he was getting tired in his legs and arms. But there was nothing to be done expect power forward, accepting their help so both Michelle and I could keep as close to the rest of the group as possible.

So many things were going through my mind—fear most of all. Though it probably took us only about an hour to go over that bridge, to me it felt way longer, with each moment fraught with potential disaster. Every time one of the trail angels came to push me, I remembered Jeff and Jack's accident the day before; I seized up, instantly locking my elbows and gripping my handlebars as hard as I could. I was fearful not only of crashing with their bike but also of falling over the concrete barrier or weaving into the line of traffic. I had worked so hard the past twenty-five years to prevent myself from getting hurt; I sure didn't want to get hurt now. To make matters worse, before I had even hit the bridge, my water pack had started to leak, and I had now run out of water.

My fears doubled as we approached the middle of the bridge. Like any bridge, there is a section that has to be taller in order for larger ships to pass through. Staring me right in the face now was a 100-foot climb of just such a section. Reaper pulled up beside me, put his hand on my back, and asked, "You see that section you have been staring at for the past mile?" I gulped and replied, "How can I miss it, Reaper? I don't know if I can do it." All the memories of times I had felt like quitting kept popping through my head. Quitting on becoming a father and a husband, not going to the gym because I just didn't want to do the workout, wanting to stop my treatments because of my headaches, and even wanting to quit having a career as an athletic trainer. I could feel my body and mind wanting to quit now, and I thought how simple it would be to roll to a stop and get off the bike.

My doubting demons haunted me front and center, and I could easily have said, "I can't do this. I have a debilitating neuromuscular disorder, and if I quit, people would totally understand—right?" When I played basketball in middle and high school and I got tired, I would always use the excuse that my knees hurt; this was before I even knew I had a disorder. Then I began thinking that no matter how I felt in this moment, I hadn't really quit my entire life—so why would I do it now?

I focused again on Michelle, who was up ahead setting an example for me, and I thought of Jeff who was riding in the same conditions with his dislocated thumb. I also thought of all the people back at home who had said, "You're doing what? No way could I do that. It sounds so exciting. You can totally do that!" I also remembered my training and the Bible verses from 1 Corinthians that meant so much to me: "All athletes are disciplined in their training. They do it to win a prize that will fade away, but we do it for an eternal prize. So I run with purpose in every step." I knew that my purpose right now was to not quit, to trust my body and God, and to keep up with my teammates.

Reaper interrupted my thoughts, saying, "Kurt, you have come this far. Just keep pedaling and don't stop. I am going to be right here with you. You've got this!" As we got closer and closer to the climb, I started praying to God. I asked him to keep me safe and get me through this. I told Reaper, "I am just going to keep my head down and pedal. Will you let me know when we get over the top?" He smiled and said, "Absolutely! LET'S GO!"

I took a deep breath, put my head down, and pedaled my feet as fast as I could without stopping for the next ten minutes (which, again, was the longest ten minutes of my life). Reaper had his hand on my back the entire time, and as we reached the top and started to come over the crest, he pushed me and said, "Now, go get Michelle and encourage her to finish strong with you."

My first thought was, I crossed my biggest hurdle! Then I realized that never in my life had I been told I was strong. Spurred on, I continued to pedal as fast as I could for the next two or three miles until I got right behind Michelle. In the distance, I caught glimpses of the rest of the group who were already at our rest stop, and I began yelling at the top of my lungs at Michelle. "Let's go, Michelle. Right there is our stop. Let's go see them." The first person to greet us as we reached the pull-off area was Robyn, and as Michelle and I rode closer, she put her hand up in the air to give us a high five.

I did it! I had conquered the hill and the longest bridge of my life. Everyone was clapping for Michelle and me. I was so happy to hear them, but I realized how thirsty I was. I asked if anyone had any extra water. Robyn walked by and, without hesitation, pulled the hose off of her Camelback, handed it to me, and said, "Take as much as you need." I drank deeply enough to take the edge off my thirst and soothe my throat from yelling. One of the other riders came over and handed me his big bottle of water and said, "Take the whole thing. I have plenty." So I downed that whole bottle, too.

Suddenly I felt dizzy, so I lay down on the ground and bent my knees up to try to get some of the blood that had been pumping through my legs back to my brain. Susan came and checked on me, and I told her what was happening. She instantly got worried and said I should probably have them come pick me up and take me to the end. I told her, "I just dominated that bridge. I'm going to finish this. I just need to get my breathing back to normal, and I will be fine." Eventually the world that was spinning around me settled, and I joined the others in getting some nutrients.

The last portion of our ride that day felt so much different than the previous forty-five miles. This time, even though I wasn't going any faster, a huge weight had been lifted off my shoulders. As we continued, I could not believe what I had just done. I kept thinking back to how I felt going over that bridge and what a relief it was to accomplish that feat—biking a seven-mile-long bridge along a four-foot-wide lane against a fifteen mph headwind next to heavy traffic. Then I got to thinking how cool a story it was, and I could not wait to tell my wife and mom what I had just done.

The next section of the journey was probably another eight to ten miles. Eventually I saw the riders ahead of me turn off the path, and I looked over to the left and saw an RV park. I asked Danny, who was riding next to me, "Is that where we are stopping for the night?" He said yes and an overwhelming sense of joy came over me. I was about to finish day two and be two-thirds of the way done with the entire adventure.

As the enormity of that sunk in, I recalled a YouTube video I had found in my research on PAF that highlighted Robyn and how the Project Athena Foundation got started. As we rolled into the last stretch going into the campsite for the night, I recalled the gist of it. Robyn said:

During the adventures, there are a lot of moments when you are questioning whether you can keep going. I see that in the Athena's face. Inside I'm saying, just wait. When you take that next step that you could not take. And then there is another 100 steps that you didn't think you could take. When you're so far over that line of what you ever understood you were capable of, all of a sudden you realize, I can do anything.

I had just taken hundreds of steps I didn't think I could take and had the same realization of awe at all I had done and could do. I had accomplished one of the hardest things I have ever had to do physically in my life. So many obstacles and roadblocks in my life I had overcome, so many hills I had climbed, so many zigs and zags I had navigated. Though this one was completely different, it was something physical that defied what a physician had told me twenty-five years ago in an MDA clinic. He said I would probably be in a wheelchair unable to walk at this stage.

So many times over the years, and the past two days, my body wanted to quit but my mind did not. I wanted to complete this for myself, and I wanted to be an example for all those people going through a health challenge and doubting they could do it, too. You can do anything if you put your mind to it. That's exactly what I did when I fought through all those hard moments: enduring the muscle biopsy that determined what condition I had, coping with the struggles of having SMA, feeling like I was a failure during my divorce, finding out I was sterile and could not give Leeann a baby just one month after getting married, surviving the pain of headaches after the first two shots, and withstanding the stress of going through those shots. The sense of all I had overcome came to a boiling point at that moment and exploded in a release of tears.

When we finally stopped, I put my feet on the ground, bent over, and laid my forearms and head on my handlebars, and continued to cry. Amanda and Reaper came over and put their hands on my shoulder and asked if I was okay. I looked at them both and all I could say was, "I just completed one of the most physically challenging things of my life." Reaper said, "HELL YA, YOU DID!!"

Eventually Robyn came over, and after I told her how I was

feeling, she gave me the biggest bear hug and placed her hand on the back of my head as a mother would comfort a child. As the others gathered around us, Robyn said, "We are all [the Gods, Goddesses, and crew] so proud of you. You want to know the best part, Kurt?"

I pulled my head off her shoulder and asked, "What?"

"We get to do this all again tomorrow," she said, then chuckled under her breath. Everyone in the group began laughing hysterically. I, too, laughed, even with tears rolling down my face.

We gathered up everybody into the vans and went for happy hour to celebrate all we had accomplished that day. That night, I had felt for the first time on the whole trip that I was part of a family with everyone with me on this trip. The bond that we had started to create was growing stronger and stronger. While there, we began playing a game Robyn called "Big Booty." The goal of the game was to make your way around the circle to the top without messing up and be crowned Big Booty. We had to call out our number and then the number of another participant's number in a rhythm, and if we missed our number or got tangled up or got out of rhythm, then we had to go to the last position in the circle and start over. At one point during the game, my number got called, and when I tried to say my number and someone else's number, I ended up mixing up them and said "Fleven" (four and eleven combined). The rest of the night, everyone was calling me Fleven.

That night at dinner, I was still riding a high. When we got back to the campgrounds, I set out my things for the next day and joined the others under one of the pavilions and had the best dinner ever— baked mahi-mahi, rice, and vegetables. I sat at a table with Sarah, Jeff, and Reaper and chatted about the day's events. The whole time, though, all I wanted was to be with my family on my birthday.

After dinner, I was mentally and physical exhausted, so I went around the tables and wished everyone a good night and headed for the door. When I got about ten feet from the door, I saw the crew walking up to me led by Zina carrying a cake lit with candles. Everyone began singing "Happy Birthday" to me. I know I had the biggest smile on my face, because even though I was not with my technical family, this family of people on this ride with me was definitely a close second. After I blew out my candles, I looked at the cake. The round cake had frosting forming the waves of the ocean; on top was a Christmas ornament of Santa Claus paddling a kayak. Written on the side of the kayak was "Big Pine Fishing Lodge," which was the name of the place we were staying that night. The ornament was removable so I could take it home with me.

Zina told me that when they had reached the campsite, she went looking for something to crown the cake, and that ornament hit her right in the face, and she knew it was going on the cake. She didn't know that my wife is a big Christmas person and loves getting ornaments that represent a time in our lives. I knew this ornament would be put in a special place and would remind me of this day. I could not have asked for anything better for my birthday.

The overjoyed feeling was flowing through my body. After dinner that night, I walked down to the water's edge by myself where I sat down on the sand near the campsites watching the moon reflect off the ocean. It was at that moment that I knew that this day had changed my life, but I was not totally sure how as of yet.

It reminded me of a movie called "Iron Cowboy: The Story of the 50.50.50." The Iron Cowboy got his name because during one of his many pursuits of finishing an Ironman competition (2.4-mile swim, 112-mile bike, then a full marathon of 26.2 miles), he dawned a cowboy hat during the race he was in, and at that moment, he was known as the Iron Cowboy. In his pursuit to complete fifty Ironman races in fifty states in fifty days while trying raise money for childhood obesity and raise awareness of this condition, he hit a brick wall at day thirty. Not only was his body starting to shut down due to lack of sleep, fatigue, and the amount of miles he had put on his body, but the fundraising part of his journey and his goal of reaching one million dollars had only come to a peak at $10,000 in thirty days.

While on his bike ride in Connecticut, he collapsed on the side of the road with the weight of what he was doing and was unsure if he could continue. He looked back on why he was doing this—to show his kids what real strength is about. His daughter, when she found out that her dad was doing fifty Ironman races, told him that she would do fifty 5 kms with him and he had an appt at 7 p.m. to run his daughter's 5 km with her.

He said this was a turning point in this whole experience. His purpose was to show to his daughter who was waiting for him that night ready to run a 5 km race with her dad. It was at that point all the complaining and frustration left him because his purpose was to show his daughter how strong he was, not to show off how much fundraising and fame he was getting from doing this amazing feat. Once he got back on his bike, he left all that emotion and frustration behind him so that he could make it by seven for a light 3.1 mile jog with his daughter. Once that weight was lifted off of him, the rest of the trip changed. The crew saw the change in him which took a lot of the stress off of them. He became more relaxed and just started to enjoy the journey he was on. He felt, at that moment of complete vulnerability, the true Iron Cowboy came alive.

As I sat along the side of that ocean thinking of what my day had brought, though our situations were different, the demons we both felt during our situations were very similar. My life was changing, and I needed something to commemorate it. My alter ego was emerging. I would forever be known to my new Project Athena family as "Fleven."

"Be Brave" coins we got at the beginning of Day 2.

Me and Nicole on day two kayaking in the
middle of the Atlantic Ocean.

Me at a break after crossing the seven-mile bridge, trying to get the world to stop spinning around me as I refueled and drank some water.

The moment I pulled into the camp site on Day 2, Robyn Benincassa coming over and giving me the biggest bear hug. The day I knew my life had changed.

Florida Keys to Adventure team on the bridge to nowhere after Day 2.

Me playing Big Booty and screwing up who I was trying to call out. Instead of saying "Number Eleven, Number Four," I said, "Fleven." This was the birth of my nickname "Fleven" came to life.

Danny and "Reaper" standing on the bridge to nowhere.

My 44th birthday cake. One of my best birthdays ever!!

The sunset after day two near our campsite in the Keys.

CHAPTER 18

DAY THREE

YOU WOULD THINK THAT AFTER SUCH AN AMAZING DAY and how tired I was that I would have slept like a baby. But let's be realistic. I was in a tent, on the ground, and not in a bed. Plus, I kept looking at the pictures I had taken the day before, trying to make sure I would never forget my experience. I got up the third day realizing that my butt crack was super raw from wearing underwear under my bike shorts. Now, a few people had told me this was one of the things I should not do, but it just seemed gross not to wear underwear. But today was the last day I would be wearing the bike shorts, so I decided to go commando.

I had heard some of the crew talking about Butt Paste, which would help with my situation, so when I got to breakfast, I discreetly asked them about it and quietly mentioned I wasn't wearing any underwear today, hoping no one would hear me. But, of course, someone did. Yep, Sarah with her super hearing. Her first sounds were, "Bow-chicka-wow-wow!" We all began laughing, and I realized how comfortable I felt around these people even after such a short time—they were family like the athletes I'd known and worked with in high school and college.

Later we gathered up our bikes, got our gear set up for the day, and met at the front entrance to the campground for the final morning sermon from Robyn.

She started by quoting Theodore Roosevelt:

"It is not the critic who counts; not the man who points out how the strong man stumbles, or where the doer of deeds could have done them better. The credit belongs to the man who is actually in the arena, whose face is marred by dust and sweat and blood; who strives valiantly; who errs, who comes short again and again, because there is no effort without error and shortcoming; but who does actually strive to do the deeds; who knows great enthusiasms, the great devotions; who spends himself in a worthy cause; who at the best knows in the end the triumph of high achievement, and who at the worst, if he fails, at least fails while daring greatly, so that his place shall never be with those cold and timid souls who neither know victory nor defeat."

Being in the Arena

We are going into the arena again today, team. One mind and one heart. Spending ourselves for a worthy cause and for great devotions to one another and to ourselves. There is no life outside of one that dares greatly, loves large, and gives freely. We get into the arena every day for many reasons and come out marred by dust and sweat and blood (and sand). But yet we go in. Day in and day out. Because that is who we are and what we do as Gods, Goddesses, Athenas, and Zeuses! Today is going to be another battle, against fatigue, soreness, lactic acid, blisters, electrolyte depletion, and on occasion, lacking the motivation to make it all the way to Key West. But the beauty of this battle is that it is one we have chosen and not one that has chosen us. We paddle and ride today for all Athenas and Zeuses who are dreaming of that moment when their feet can touch the sand again, their paddles can touch the ocean again, and they can be 'free' of the fear, and the pain, and the wondering. Being an Athena or Zeus (and/or a Goddess/God) doesn't mean getting back to what you WERE, but boldly and confidently moving forward into what you ARE . . . embracing what you CAN do, and most important, surrounding yourself with loving and inspiring people who believe. THAT is what today is all about. Showing yourself, one another, and our future Athenas and Zeuses that you believe that anything is possible, no matter the setbacks, no matter the odds, no matter the fatigue, no matter the fear.

Let's get into that arena one more time, gang. For ourselves, our future Athenas and Zeuses, and for our friends and family who can't wait to hear that their favorite Goddess or God has touched the southernmost tip of the USA in Key West!

After Robyn's rousing speech, we all were given carabiners with our names written on them. The carabiners were symbols of whatever hooks you into your lifeline. These clips are used by mountain climbers to hook into their ropes as they are repelling or ascending a cliff; they also can clip necessary items such as water bottles into athletes' belts so they have access to them but can keep their hands free. And they create a supportive lifeline where you can clasp onto another person when you or they are struggling.

She always told us we are only as successful and strong as our weakest/slowest person. In the numerous eco-challenge races Robyn completed, she learned during parts of the competitions that it was best for the whole team to hook onto each other's harnesses and ropes so all were connected to take the pressure off the slower person.

So many things in life are like this. We surround ourselves with people who have the same interests we do. We marry a partner who is there in life to have our back, not only in bad times but also when we need someone to help and encourage us—and we do the same for them. Even more important, this is what God does for us. This was the kind of support I had been searching for as I stepped through life.

It reminds me of the poem "Footprints in the Sand." Here's one version of this anonymous prayer:

One night I had a dream . . .
I dreamed I was walking along the beach with the Lord
And across the sky flashed scenes from my life.
For each scene I noticed two sets of footprints in the sand;
One belonged to me, and the other to the Lord.
When the last scene of my life flashed before us,
I looked back at the footprints in the sand.

I noticed that many times along the path of my life,

There was only one set of footprints.

I also noticed that it happened at the very lowest and saddest
times in my life.

This really bothered me, and I questioned the Lord about it.

"Lord, you said that once I decided to follow you,

You would walk with me all the way;

But I have noticed that during the most troublesome times in
my life,

There is only one set of footprints.

I don't understand why in times when I needed you the most,

You should leave me."

The Lord replied, "My precious, precious child.

I love you, and I would never, never leave you

during your times of trial and suffering.

When you saw only one set of footprints,

It was then that I carried you."

God is our permanent, omnipresent carabiner. He always has a
clip on us for support as long as we follow him. And the carabiner
helps me to remember how God and other people carry us—and
we are never alone.

I had noticed over the past two days on Robyn's Camelback
water pack that she had pictures attached with carabiners. Over
the time she has been doing these adventures, she has experienced
numerous Athenas, Zeuses, Gods, and Goddesses who have, as she
so perfectly puts it, gained their angel wings and passed on. She
wears their pictures on every adventure, so they are still with the
group keeping us safe and pulling us along.

We were told that third morning we needed to exchange our carabiner with someone else in the group. I did not hesitate and went over to Jeff who had dislocated his thumb in the accident in the storm. He had been one of my main motivators pulling me just the day before, over that bridge, because I knew he was ahead of me, and I thought, if he wasn't going to quit, I wasn't either. To this day when I look at that carabiner, I think of the energy of being connected to other inspiring people getting me to the finish line. And I think of God giving me a pull to the finish line on Earth, and the heavenly finish line I'll one day cross when I earn my own angel wings.

We all gathered up our things and began our journey to the finish line in front of us that day to Key West. Seeing the early morning sun rising as we were biking across the bridges and along the shoreline of the Atlantic Ocean was amazing. But what would be hitting me in the face yet again? Yep, that stupid fifteen mph headwind.

Fortunately, a short ten-mile ride later, we pulled into a boat area where the crew was waiting for us to transition to the kayaks. We had the opportunity to change and get some snacks, then we all came together and Robyn paired us up for the last kayak ride of the adventure. During training, Amanda, our training coach, and I had talked about hoping we were teamed together one of the days. As soon as Robyn looked at me on day three, I got excited and asked, "Can I get Amanda?" She thought for a second and said, "Yes. Go ahead." It kind of reminded me of a mother telling her kid to go ahead and take the last cookie out of the jar before a meal or bedtime. For me, Amanda was my special treat.

Amanda had been sharing a double kayak with Chenier and Jeff the previous two days. We had not had the best days in the water, with the wind and waves hitting us from every direction. She also had been riding on one of the tandem bikes with Sarah, so Amanda had been working her butt off during this trip. A hole in one of the kayaks had to be patched up, but then we headed from the cove area, which was surrounded by beautiful homes with boats galore lining the shore and out to the ocean.

Once we hit the open ocean, we all noticed how different things seemed. Not only was the sun out, but the waves also were coming from behind us, along with a sweet tailwind that pushed us forward in the direction we were supposed to go—for once. I looked back at Amanda and asked how she was doing. She said, with the biggest smile on her face, "This has to be the best leg of the entire trip for me for sure. This unicorn has been on the struggle bus the last couple days, and finally I get a kick in my step with a great partner to kayak with me today." We both started to laugh.

I learned driving from the airport to Key Largo that Amanda and Zina were huge fans of unicorns. Robyn's birthday was the day before our first day, so the crew had gotten her a cake with a unicorn horn on it. Of course, Amanda taped that unicorn horn to the top of her bike helmet and wore it the entire trip. I found myself wishing that leg of the kayaking would never end, because in addition to not having to worry about getting tipped over, we all were able to stay close in a pack. Being able to talk to some of the other kayakers was fun and rewarding, and we could really take in the beautiful coast of South Florida.

Halfway through the leg, we noticed these buoys scattered randomly in the water. I think they were there to indicate the crab pots below them. The water was so clear we could see the seaweed and the sand at the bottom of the ocean, so we made a game out of racing to see if we could hit a buoy straight on with our kayaks. It got pretty competitive among many of the boats, but it was all in lighthearted fun.

We finally made it into this narrow bay area where the wind was pulling the waves straight at the front of our kayaks. It was fun going up and down like a roller coaster in the swells as the waves moved us and water splashed over the bows of the boats. I paddled constantly to get out of this spot as quickly as possible, but numerous times, I moved to stick my oar in the water only to find we were at the top of the wave, causing my oar to skip off the water ineffectually into the air. I kept checking on Amanda, and her fun meter was droppings as quickly as mine was rising. Soon we entered the cove where were met the land crew. I realized that would be the last day I would be able to kayak in the ocean. That was our longest trip in the ocean, with 13.5 miles traveled, but it had been the most perfect.

We were told there was a bar area with food for us all and to meet up in about twenty-five minutes on our bikes for the final leg of the adventure. We walked around to this amazing open-air bar that overlooked the bay right on the water's edge. On the table was a great spread of calamari, fried perch, onion rings, chicken wings, and even some beef nachos. It was so enticing that without even thinking about washing our hands first, we grabbed food and started eating it. Somehow, after indulging in a ton of food, we changed clothes and gathered up our bikes.

This last leg on the bike I remember as if it were yesterday. All I wanted to do was take in the scenery so I could remember what everything looked like. Too soon for me, we covered the many turns and bridges that took us into Key West. We had finally made it.

As we rode along the coast, we could see the different ships out in the ocean and the white sandy beaches that lined the path we were riding on in the outskirts of town. The streets were packed with tourists and locals walking along. It reminded me of all those races I had covered the past years in Toledo, where the people would sit in their driveways holding up encouraging signs or stand along the streets trying to catch glimpses of their friend, mom, dad, brother, or sister running. Even though there were no cops holding back traffic or barriers to stop cars and people from crossing in front of us, it felt like we were the only ones on the road. We were just riding in the middle of the road in our group.

Riding through the inner portion of town, we saw some of the most beautiful historical houses with grand sidewalks and yards in pristine condition. Turning down the final road, we began noticing more and more people gathering along the side of the road. Most of them were headed, as we were, to the anchored concrete buoy, a historical landmark, that marks the southernmost point of the United States. It sports multiple stripes of red, yellow, and blue and words in various colors pointing out where it is and mentioning the spot is only ninety miles from Cuba.

As we road toward the landmark, people began cheering us on, sending chills down my spine as I remembered the cheering crowds in those races I had worked. That none of these people knew where we were from or that we had come 120 miles to get here didn't really matter to me. It was something that I had envisioned would happen when I dreamed of finishing a race. A race that until this point I had never done, due to fear of failing, fear of hurting myself, and fear of not being able to finish. We eventually made it to the landmark and parked our bikes along the side of the fence overlooking the ocean. There were at least fifty people waiting in line to take their picture in front of the buoy. I thought, we're going to be here a while. Then

Robyn gathered us all together and told us we were going to sneak up near the buoy, and when she gave us the signal, we were all going to rush it, take a quick picture, and get out of there. So we did. Then we headed back to the beach to finish up.

The ride back to the beach was the easiest of the entire trip. I thought back on all the things I had been through on that trip, the highs and lows I had experienced over the three days, including the demons I had fought that wanted me to quit. But I had not quit even then, and I did not quit now. Eventually we rolled up to a fenced area near a tennis court where our bike trailer was. I thought to myself that this was the end; it was over. Everyone gathered their things and headed to the beach. I looked out along the walking path that led to the inlet.

We gathered on the sand and Robyn gave her final speech:

Your Mission as Gods/Goddesses and Athenas/Zeuses!

We made it to Key West! It's been a beautiful few days in our little cocoon of aspiration and inspiration, hasn't it? Many of us, including me, wish that it would never end. And some of us are pretty sure it ended just in time. But crossing this finish line and reaching the southernmost part of the United States is not really the end. Your mission now is to share with our friends and family what we feel in our hearts (hands, shoulders, legs, bike seat area) and to inspire others to be the very best they can be, to strive for what is important to them, to help them appreciate even more how fleeting and heartbreakingly beautiful life is, to be healthy and strong, to love themselves, to get rid of the roadblocks in their life, to rise to the challenges time and time again, to be grateful for every moment that we have here with one another, and to remember that the good stuff in life sometimes lies in the struggles—because it is in those times of struggle, when the universe extends its hand and invites us to rise to the occasion, that we discover how amazing and beautiful and strong we truly are.

So inspire those around you to get into the arena every day. And remind yourself every morning that life is too short to live in that gray twilight that knows neither victory nor defeat. Take risks, love big, fail often (for failure paves the way to success, brick by brick), and inspire and amaze yourself each day (because being inspired is an INSIDE job). And when you have those moments of doubt, remember US. Remember THIS. Remember how awesome and exhausted and sandy and victorious you are right now. In this moment. And keep this feeling locked away in your mind and in your heart. You are an endurance athlete. You are a Goddess, you are an Athena, you are a Zeus. And you have proved to yourself and the teammates around you that, in the infamous words of Christopher Robin, "You are braver than you believe, and stronger than you seem, and smarter than you think."

Here's to you. And to the next huge, hairy, audacious goals you have in your life. And to building a team of Gods and Goddesses around you that will push, pull, tug, and tow each other every inch of the way!

As she finished her speech, she pointed down the beach and said, "Now, there is your finish line. GO GET IT!" I peered down the beach and for the first time in my life I saw a finish line for a race I never knew was possible for me to ever do was staring me in the face. Jeff, Britney, and I joined hands, then Chenier and Sarah (a God and Goddess on this trip), who had been an Athena and Zeus on previous events, stood on either side of us, and we all five walked together down the beach, savoring each step. I was realizing the dream I'd had almost a year to the day, when I had called Susan and asked her if it would be okay for me to do a race, and she had told me about Project Athena. The finish line that I had watched so many people cross over the years at cross-country meets and other races was in sight for me—the line represented the countless number of victories I had watched, victories that were achieved because of all the training and mental preparation. This time, this victory was mine, made possible by me—I was not alone, but it was up to me to do the work.

The Trail Angel Crew had a banner draped across the beach as our finish line. As we walked across the sand, I felt the softness under my feet with each step forward. I was holding the hand of a man with a deteriorating blindness disease and a freshly dislocated thumb and the hand of a young lady who had kicked cancer's butt just one year ago. There I was in the middle. A little nobody from Muncie, Indiana, who grew up with a vision of what his life and future would look like, but who got diagnosed with a rare form of muscular dystrophy that should have put him in a wheelchair by the time he was thirty-five. A guy who fought through that and so many other things to get to this point. He, I, was crossing the finish line after biking and kayaking about 120 miles from Key Largo to Key West.

Each of us raised our hands in victory as we passed under the banner then gave each other hugs.

There was one special person I was eager to see, and that was Susan. I scanned the faces of all of the participants and spotted her. As soon as we caught each other's eyes, we both started crying. We hugged each other, and I thanked her for getting me involved with Project Athena and supporting me and my family with my treatment and training. My gratitude was greater than I could say, but I know she understands.

After our congratulations wound down, we made our way to a pavilion and partook of champagne in red SOLO cups. Before I took even one sip, I felt buoyant and lighthearted. We gathered in a circle then went around and shared what we were feeling. I listened to everyone talk about their experiences. The topic of how sore our butts were was at the top of most people's lists. I was glad I was close to the last person because it took that long for me to realize exactly what I was feeling.

I said the weight of so much fear, doubt, frustration, and fear had been lifted off my shoulders, and I thanked Blain (Reaper) and Danny for all their help. I also said that there were so many times on the bridge the day before that I wanted to quit, but because of Michelle and Jeff still up there riding, I knew that I couldn't. I mentioned that if it was not for Susan doing this race a week before I called her, I would not be here. And if it was not for the drug I had been put on for my SMA and the decrease in fatigue, I would not have had the courage to even try something like this.

I explained that after being diagnosed, I gave up sports out of fear of getting hurt and to make sure I was healthy enough to pursue a career that my first neurologist told me I should not pursue. I also gave up sports so I could spend my time in the weight room six days a week for twenty-five years. But now, and for the first time in my life, I finally figured out what I had been searching for and was missing, something I had stuffed so far down deep inside of me, I'd forgotten it was even there. It was being an athlete. Now I feel like an athlete again.

I used to tell people when I was at the gym that lifting to make myself better each and every day was my sport. That was my challenge. I thought going to the gym was my goal and purpose, but it wasn't. My purpose was developing and sharing the qualities and essence of being an athlete who strives for excellence and embodies the highest ideals of competition to complete the race of life, and who trusts in God, teammates, and loved ones to be there every step of the way.

After I finished thanking everyone, Robyn said, "Kurt, you can now officially call yourself a world-class endurance athlete!"

I thought, *What did she just say?* She called me not just a normal athlete but an endurance athlete. I had gone the distance stretching back twenty-five years and earlier, with each step getting me closer to finding and sharing my purpose. For so many years, I had carried this heavy weighted chain around my neck. A weight of doubt of where my life would take me. A weight of insecurity: would I be able to be in a career that I wanted to be in, and would I be able to do my job to the best of my ability with a disability? A lack of hope of how long I would be able to postpone being in a wheelchair. The weight of insecurity of being judged for having a disability. The fear of hurting myself and losing my ability to walk.

That weight of doubt about who I am was lifted off my shoulders and slammed to the ground with that one simple phrase. It was the best feeling in the world and, of course, I was crying happy tears the entire time.

Robyn came over and placed my finishing medal around my neck, something I had wanted of my own since I was a kid. I had gotten medals and rings as part of the medical team with a sport while I was in college, but never for something I had earned on my own. I remembered all the teams I had seen making it to the state high school championship game and receiving medals. I thought of all those races I covered where, after they crossed the finish line, the participants proudly wore their medals around their necks showing they had finished an audacious race. I had never had one—until now.

I looked down at that medal. One side had the Project Athena logo and the other side said, "120ish Florida Keys to Recovery Finisher."

I, debilitating neurological disease and all, Kurt Beach, a finisher. I had accomplished something no one thought I would be able to do. I had done it. That chain of doubt that I had been carrying for almost twenty-five years was replaced with a chain of assurance of where my life will be, no insecurities, hope, and no fear.

The whole crew in front of the southernmost tip of
the continental United States buoy in Key West.

The whole group crossing the finish line on day three near the
tip of Key West with Barney (Cheniers' dog) waiting for his
owner. Barney became an honorary PAF crew for the week.

Me crossing the finish line with two other Athenas/Zueuses and two Gods/Goddesses on the last day near the southern-most point in the continental United States in Key West, FL.

Me finding Susan Haverland after crossing the finish line on day three near the tip of Key West. You're welcome, Susan, for not putting the picture of your ugly crying.

Me getting my medal, Zeus headdress, and 120ish mile sticker to place on my car. First ever race sticker I have ever put on my car.

EPILOGUE

I CAN READ ROBYN'S DAY-THREE SPEECH over and over again, and it never gets old and still sends chills and goosebumps over my body, especially the Theodore Roosevelt quote about being in the arena, "face marred by dust and sweat and blood; who strives valiantly; who errs, who comes short again and again … [yet] daring greatly, so that his place shall never be with those cold and timid souls who neither know victory nor defeat."

That is what it has been like for me for over half my life since getting diagnosed with SMA at a young age. I have been a Zeus my whole life. I set out from day one with blood, sweat, and even some tears along the way and hit the gym six days a week with rarely a break except Sundays, because we all know even God gave himself a day of rest. Did I stumble many times over all those years? Absolutely. Did I fail at times? Yes, both literally and figuratively. But I never gave up because I had a goal each and every day I was in the gym (arena), and that was to make myself better than I was the day before. There have been plenty of shortcomings, not only with my condition but also throughout my life, but those battles have made me the person I am today.

My SMA battle chose me; I did not choose it. But only I could choose the path this battle would take me down. Every day is a struggle, but every day I choose to continue the fight. I fight so that my feet can walk across the sand and pedal the bike and my arms can paddle the kayak—all to give me confidence in walking the days of my life to the fullest. The important word is "walk."

My fear has always been losing my ability to walk. I want to walk, but not just so I can work or be independent and not be a strain on my wife; it's way more than that. I want to be able to stand and throw a ball with my son in the backyard when he gets older and be able to walk my daughter down the aisle and dance with her at her wedding.

All Zeuses and Athenas are people who have had a medical setback in their lives, but no matter the fear, the fatigue, or the odds, we have kept putting one foot forward, entering the arena of our lives, and daring greatly.

This is also the life of my faith as I searched with every step for spiritual purpose. I wrote Robyn a few days after the event was over:

I keep thinking of all the things I have brought out of this whole experience. I will never forget your speech on day two about being brave and getting the carabiners on day three. Throughout my life, I have always been fearful of hurting myself, because if I did, I would have a setback. The whole time Reaper was helping me get past those sticking points and pushing me up those more difficult spots along the path, I had a death grip on my handlebars with the fear of crashing. But through that fear, I developed a trust with him and Danny. I think that is what God is there to do with us. To give us a push when we are fearful and know that all we need to do is trust him.

Coming back from the Keys, I felt like a completely different person. For nearly a quarter of a century, I had been searching for my next step. Sometimes there was anger, and I would be lying if I said there was not a little bit of bitterness thrown in with some of my steps. I also had some worry about which step might be my last.

The idea that the cross is a sign of hope is only part of the picture. In fact, the cross is the sign of death and suffering. Jesus carried that cross and took many grueling steps up the hill of Golgotha where he was crucified. With every step he took, he carried that heavy wooden cross with the purpose of ridding the world of sin. Before his crucifixion, in the Garden of Gethsemane, Jesus prayed to God: "My Father, if it is possible, may this cup be taken from me. Yet not as I will, but as you will" (Matthew 26:42 NIV). Knowing what he would have to do to finish his journey, Jesus wanted to make sure it truly was God's will.

For me, I found Jesus at the early stages of my diagnosis. I remember one day while riding my bike in the countryside around Muncie, Indiana, praying this exact prayer: "Jesus, please take this burden of SMA away from me. But if this is what you will have for me, please let your will be done through it." For many years I carried that burden, and I took every step searching for where my next one would come. It took me twenty-five years to figure out what God wanted to do with me with this disability.

I did not know where each next step would lead me—there were many joys throughout my life but also a lot of suffering. But through that suffering, I felt like God gave me the strength I needed to take so many steps in my life. If it were not for those burdens, I would not have found what my sole purpose in life is: To show people that life throws obstacles in your way, and those obstacles show you the strength God has. God put people in my life to show me there is hope.

He also put many people in my life to show me what life was about and how to cope with having a disability. God gave me Coach Walters (my golf coach) to show me that if I focus on a goal and stay the course that I could be successful in whatever I do. God put Nate Wessel in my life to show me that what people have on the outside does not always show the strength and fortitude they have on the inside. God showed me through Beth Scott that people with disabilities can live a full life just like anyone else. He gave me Gary Ream at Camp Woodward to show me the strengths I had as an athletic trainer; I just needed a place I could let them shine. He gave me Rex Stump to show me that even in the rough times in life and even with the simplest request, God is there for me and is listening. God gave me a daughter, and a son, so I could show her that inner strength outweighs the strength we have on the surface. He gave me Susan Haverland, who would be the person, when I was looking for a hook, to finally pull me out of the water and give me the courage to tell me I could do an athletic event. God gave me Robyn Benincasa and the Project Athena Foundation to show me the light I had inside of me, and that I just needed a new supercharged battery to replace the worn-out one.

He gave me my wife, Leeann, to show me the love I never knew I deserved and show me that someone with a disability can be loved for who they are on the inside. And he put my parents in my life to show me that no matter how hard I might fall or how much pain or hurt I might have at any given time, just like God, my parents would always be there to pick me up.

After the Keys, I figured out what the purpose in my steps was. My purpose was to show the strength, though lacking sometimes on the outside in the physical body, I have on the inside (the mental strength)—because of having to wrestle with those physical short-comings. My purpose also was to show others the power that God has when you just believe in him and have faith he will guide you in every step you take.

After finishing the event, I was not sure I wanted to do the Keys event again, but I knew I wanted to enter more races. As I thought further about doing something once and not trying to do it again, it didn't feel right. So on the third day back, I signed up for the Keys to Recovery again, coming back as a God (fund raiser). The decision was a pretty simple decision for two reasons. One was knowing there were no races as beautiful as going through the Keys in Florida. The second reason was I wanted to pay the support I had received forward to someone else, to be able to flip their setback into a come-back, as the Gods and Goddesses had done for me. I also now knew I could go thirty miles in one day because I had just done 120 in three days. So I decided to join one of my teachers at Springfield, whose wife suffers from multiple sclerosis, for a race in Toledo called the Bike to the Bay (seventy-five miles). I returned to the Keys in 2020, and then in April 2021, I finally crossed the finish line for my first-ever 5 km race with my daughter walking next to me.

Since the race in November 2019 and through telling my story to the people I work with and the kids at Springfield High, I am noticing a different person inside myself. Releasing the weight at the finish line in Key West changed who I was as a person. For the most part, the fear of hurting myself, the fear of people judging me for my disability, and the fear of being permanently stuck in a wheelchair for the rest of my life are gone. I no longer need to fear being hurt because I know all I have to do is put the work in to get better, and I know God will be there with me. I do not need to worry about people judging me for my disability, because I have done something few could even fathom being able to do.

Training for, striving in, then crossing the finish showed me my inner athlete as well as my connection with teammates and God. I learned to not take Jesus in my life for granted. I know he is here but sometimes he gets pushed way down deep inside. But when I begin to let that fear or hesitancy loose and really believe and commit myself to him, the true meaning of life and being a Christian athlete is made manifest and the miracles begin.

As Robyn says, "Go and show the world the light that you have deep inside you." On my second trip to the Keys in 2020, I saw a picture of myself from the first day of that trip. The comments everyone kept posting were about how bright my smile was and how they bet I smiled in my sleep. It kind of gave me a complex: do I really smile that much or was I just smiling more than normal? I was curious since few people had ever commented on my smile before. But then I went back and looked at my day-one picture from the 2019 trip. I realized that was a different person and a different smile.

I now see a guy who has pushed fear and uncertainty aside. I see a guy who wants to take full advantage of this new lease on life that God has given him. I see the light that Robyn talks about so much in her pre-race sermons, the light we have inside of us that we are meant to find and share. In that light, I see hope of a future I am living in.

So, yes, I may sleep at night with a smile on my face. I know it is the smile I was searching for all along. And it promises that I am someone who wants to take full advantage of every opportunity I have to challenge myself and help others do the same. Step-by-step, with purpose in every step.

ABOUT THE AUTHOR

KURT BEACH is currently the athletic trainer at Springfield High School in Holland, Ohio. He lives in Perrysburg, Ohio, with his wife and two children. He continues to participate with the Project Athena Foundation and competes in other local races in the area as well. He currently attends Calvary Church and is involved in the Cure SMA community to fight for the rights of adults with spinal muscular atrophy and raise awareness of the condition and the treatment for it. He is also in the process of starting his own non-profit to help individuals with SMA and their families get the proper equipment they need not only to survive but also to develop their strength, both mentally and physically, with the hope that they are able to join him in a race someday.

Made in the USA
Monee, IL
19 October 2021